BATTL
GUIDE
VERDUN
1916

BATTLEFIELD GUIDE SERIES

A series of guides to the key battles of the First and Second World Wars that marries expert narrative from leading military historians to a highly detailed guide to the battlefield today. Richly illustrated with contemporary and current photographs, maps and local information, they are an invaluable tool for the series military reader and the battlefield visitor alike.

Series Editor

An expert on the First and Second World Wars, William F. Buckingham holds a PhD in military history and teaches history at the University of Glasgow. His other books include the launch title in this series *Verdun 1916*, *D-Day: The First 72 Hours*, *Arnhem 1944* and *Paras*.

Forthcoming Titles

The Somme
Arras
Ypres
D-Day
Arnhem
The Battle of the Bulge

BATTLEFIELD
GUIDE
VERDUN
1916

WILLIAM F. BUCKINGHAM

TEMPUS

First published 2007

Tempus Publishing Limited
The Mill, Brimscombe Port,
Stroud, Gloucestershire, GL5 2QG
www.tempus-publishing.com

British Library Cataloguing in Publication Data.
A catalogue record for this book is available from the British Library.

ISBN 978 07524 4148 1

Typesetting and origination by Tempus Publishing Limited
Printed and bound in Great Britain

Contents

Introduction

The 1916 Battle of Verdun is widely regarded as a uniquely awful low point in a conflict that was by no means short of such woeful milestones. The very name has become synonymous with pyrrhic victory won at horrific cost, as exemplified by the tag 'Verdun on the Volga' applied to the battle for Stalingrad twenty-six years later in a different war. This reputation is not simply due to casualty figures, which are notoriously difficult to pin down with certainty. The combined figure of around 681,000 French and German killed, wounded and missing at Verdun is only around half that for the 1916 Battle of the Somme, which racked up a combined British, French and German casualty toll of somewhere between 1.1 and 1.3 million.

Despite this, Verdun's reputation as the worst of the worst is well deserved. The Battle of the Somme lasted for just over four months, whilst Verdun ground on for over five months before the Germans finally abandoned their offensive, and nine months if the French counter-offensives that restored their line to something like the pre-battle status quo are included. The nearest British equivalent to this longevity was the dogged occupation of the Ypres Salient, but that particular Calvary was overwhelmingly a matter of sitting and taking whatever the Germans chose to dish out rather than withstanding months of heavy and sustained attack followed by sustained counter-attack. Unlike its British counterparts, the battle for Verdun also had the potential to make or break the Allied war effort. Had the Germans succeeded in breaking through to Verdun, as they almost did in February and July 1916, there would have been little between them and Paris. The loss of the French capital might well have been sufficient to knock France out of the war as the architect of the German plan predicted.

Be that as it may, the intensity of the fighting at Verdun was also more tightly focussed. The original attack frontage at Verdun was approximately eight miles wide, only half that of the Somme, and in the later climactic stages of the German offensive at Verdun in July 1916 entire corps were being compressed into attack frontages of three miles or less. By that time the Germans had abandoned any pretence of tactical finesse and were simply trying to bludgeon through the French defence by sheer weight of numbers, with a density of a man for every metre of front. The result of such 'tactics' in the face of modern weaponry can be easily imagined, and the battle left an indelible mark on the French too. Their *noria* replacement system meant that seventy of the ninety-six French divisions on the Western Front passed through what became dubbed 'the mill on the Meuse', and the deleterious effects of this exposure lay at the root of the widespread mutiny that gripped the French Army from April 1917.

However, the most graphic evidence to support Verdun's unenviable status is the physical scar the battle has left on the ground over which it was fought. With the exception of a handful of fragments, such as Sanctuary Wood near Ypres and the Memorial Parks at Vimy and Beaumont Hamel on the Somme, there is little trace of the monumental struggle that took place along a 400-mile strip of Belgium and France. Without the immaculately maintained military graveyards, memorials and occasional museum there would be no clue at all. The exception to this is Verdun, where, apart from large-scale conifer planting and the erection of memorials, almost 200 square kilometres have been left largely in the state they were in 1918. This was not generally a deliberate policy, but was obliged by the fact that the intensity of the fighting had literally blasted away the topsoil and poisoned the ground to an extent that defied post-war attempts to return it to former use. Thus the conifer plantations that now blanket the battlefield preserve a moonscape of shell craters, trenches and the crumbling remains of permanent fortifications like Fort Vaux, the scene of hellish underground fighting of a type that occurred nowhere else on the Western Front.

This book is divided into two sections. The first is a concise account of the 1916 Battle of Verdun, illustrated with contemporary photographs and maps, with a potted history of the town and additional background information to put the battle into its proper context. The second section is a guide to the battlefield today with details of how to reach Verdun, illustrated with current photographs taken by the author and the words of soldiers who actually fought on the ground described. This is backed with a guide to further reading and a list of websites containing additional information for the student of the battle and prospective tourist alike. The author has visited Verdun sixteen times since 1989, sometimes to visit specific areas of the battlefield, and sometimes en route to or from elsewhere as the town makes a conveniently placed stopover point. Hopefully this work will prompt some readers to visit Verdun and the adjacent battlefield and experience the unique landscape and atmosphere for themselves.

William F. Buckingham
Bishopbriggs, Glasgow
April 2006

PART 1

Verdun: The Battle

Verdun the Fortress Town: 450 BC–1914

Verdun is a typical small French provincial town, located on a steep bluff overlooking a crossing on the River Meuse, 140 miles east of Paris. Before the monumental bloodletting between February and December 1916, the town's main claim to fame was as a trading centre for eunuchs and the ongoing production of sugared almonds, a confection originally produced in the Middle Ages at the behest of the local apothecary's guild.[1] To the west, the wooded ridges of the Argonne gradually subside into a rolling chalk plain dominated by the cathedral city of Reims. To the east, the town is overlooked by the long, heavily wooded ridge of the Meuse Heights. The ridge parallels the Meuse before merging into a series of similar ridges, intercut with steep ravines running down to the river, that undulate north for forty miles or so into the semi-mountainous Ardennes. The Heights give way in turn to a low-lying plain cut by numerous watercourses and dotted with woods and small lakes, stretching the thirty miles further east to Metz and the River Moselle.

The site of the town was named Virodunum (roughly 'the fortress that controls the river crossing') by the Celtic tribesmen who occupied it from 450 BC to 57 BC, when they were supplanted by the Romans. By the fourth century AD Virodunensium had expanded from a Roman military fort into a prosperous civil settlement, thanks to its key location on the road between Reims and Metz. The town was sacked by Attila's Huns in 450 AD, and Verdun's first cathedral was built during the subsequent reconstruction. In 843 the Treaty of Verdun divided the Carolingian Empire among Charlemagne's sons, and Verdun began its 1,273 year stint as a Gallo-Germanic bone of contention. Initially assigned to the short-lived Middle Kingdom, Verdun was incorporated into the Eastern Empire in 923 and remained in the Germanic sphere of influence until 1552. In that year Henri II of France acquired Verdun, Metz and Toul from Emperor Charles V via some diplomatic sleight of hand. Verdun thus passed back into French hands, although the Germanic claim was not abandoned until the Treaty of Münster formally acknowledged French sovereignty in 1648.

Verdun's defensive walls were reworked between 1567 and 1591 in expectation of a Germanic riposte, and Marshal of France Louis de Marillac oversaw the construction of a fortified citadel atop the bluff from 1624. This marked the beginning of Verdun's transformation into a military garrison town, but the real shift came with Louis XIV's drive to round out and fortify the borders of his kingdom into the *pré carré* (enclosed domain) envisioned by Cardinal Richelieu during the reign of his father. The task of fortifying France's borders was entrusted to Louis's most eminent military engineer Sebastien Le Prestre, better known as Marshal Vauban. Vauban reviewed Verdun's defences in 1664, and over the next three decades Verdun's citadel and curtain wall were rebuilt into the standard geometric design with bastions, ravelins, interlocking fields of fire and sloping grass glacis to deflect artillery shot and slow the pace of attacking troops. A barracks to house the town garrison was completed in 1739.

Vauban's works were state of the art, but they could only be as good as those manning them. This proved to be the weak link in 1792, when Verdun was briefly besieged by Prussian troops from the force despatched by Europe's crowned heads to crush the French Revolution. The town commandant, a Colonel Beaurepaire, publicly refused to contemplate surrender but the town's citizenry displayed rather less revolutionary ardour, not least because the garrison could only muster forty-four men to man thirty-two artillery pieces, and the town's Council of Defence voted to surrender. The impasse ended with Beaurepaire's demise on 2 September 1792, either by despairing suicide or at the hands of the townspeople depending on the account. Verdun surrendered the next day, sparking riots in Paris and the massacre of a number of political prisoners, but the occupation was relatively short and the town was liberated by General Kellerman on 14 October 1792, following the French victory over the counter-revolutionary forces at Valmy the previous month.

Verdun's next major siege was a rather more honourable affair, albeit with the same ultimate outcome. Franco-German rivalry came to a head following a diplomatic dispute over who was to fill the vacant Spanish throne, and France rashly declared war on the Prussian-led North German Confederation on 19 July 1870. The optimistically dubbed 'Army of the Rhine' mobilised with some confusion and duly set out for German territory headed by Emperor Napoleon III

1 Map of Verdun before 1914, showing the geometric Vauban defence works.

in person. After capturing Saarbrücken on 2 August the French were outmanoeuvred and outfought by a Prussian counter-invasion two days later, and after suffering relatively minor defeats at Wœrth and Spicheren the French Army was split. Half, under Napoleon and Marshal Marie Edmé Patrice de MacMahon, retired north-west, while the remainder under Marshal Achille Bazaine retired on Metz; Verdun was besieged on 9 August as part of the Prussian ring around Metz. Bazaine made two abortive breakouts, at Vionville and Gravelotte on 16 and 18 August respectively, to meet a relief attempt by MacMahon. This too ended in disaster at Sedan, where the Prussians defeated MacMahon and captured Napoleon and 100,000 of his men on 1 September 1871. Bazaine and the 180,000 men in Metz held out until 27 October 1871 before capitulating, and Verdun carried on until 8 November before accepting a Prussian offer of surrender with full military honours. The town remained under occupation until 13 September 1873, when the Prussians finally withdrew.

The consequences of the events of 1870–71 impacted directly on the future of France generally and Verdun in particular. They left France facing an even more formidable foe, as Bismarck adroitly manipulated victory to create a unified Germany and acquired Alsace and Lorraine as reparations for French aggression. This shifted the Franco-German border from the Rhine to west of the Moselle, and left the Meuse as the only defensible barrier between Paris and another German invasion. The French were thus obliged to build a new set of defences along the 140 miles between the Belgian and Swiss borders, a task entrusted to an engineer general named Séré de Rivières.[2] In the decade from 1874, 166 forts and forty-three smaller works were constructed, largely by Italian immigrant labour. Anchored on Belfort in the south, the line ran along high ground to Épinal, thence to Toul and along the River Meuse to Verdun. The line was continuous apart from a forty-mile gap between Épinal and Toul, labelled the Belfort Gap or *Trouée de Charmes* (charmed gap), a wordplay on the town of that name east of Toul. The Gap was intended to channel attackers onto terrain favourable for a French counter-attack.[3]

Verdun was thus elevated from military backwater to northern anchor of the French border defences, guarding best line of advance toward Paris and the French hinterland. General de Rivières's work was augmented and updated through the 1880s and 1890s on the instructions of Minister of War Charles de Freycinet, to keep them abreast of advances in military technology, and especially artillery. Thus by 1914 Verdun was protected by nineteen forts and a similar

number of supporting fortifications, called ouvrages. Seven of the
forts were situated on the west bank of the Meuse, three directly
west of Verdun (Chaume, Sartelles and Chana), and the remainder
(Choisel, Vacherauville, Marre and Bois Bourrus) along the Bois
Bourrus Ridge, four miles north-west of the town. On the east bank,
Forts Rozellier, Moulainville and Belrupt guarded the south-eastern
and eastern approaches. The rest were distributed in two concentric
rings to the north-east, with Forts Tavannes, Souville, St Michel and
Belleville forming the inner ring. The outer ring consisted of two
forts sited on the highest points of the Meuse Ridge supported by a
number of protective works. Fort Vaux sat on a 340-metre elevation
overlooking the low lying Woëvre Plain, while Fort Douaumont was
oriented north on a 396-metre plateau a few hundred metres east
of the village of the same name.

Fort Douaumont was the keystone and showcase of Verdun's
defences. The garrison was reminded of the fact by the motto
painted on the fort's central corridor: *S'ensevelir sous les ruines du
fort plutôt que de le rendre* (rather be buried beneath the ruins of
the fort than surrender).[4] Completed in 1913 at a total cost of
6.1 million francs,[5] the fort was polygonal in plan, 250 metres to a
side. It was girdled by a dry concrete ditch with integral machine
gun galleries sited to sweep its length, the galleries being linked to
the fort by tunnels. The ditch was also screened by metal railings,
aprons of barbed wire and supporting fortifications. Douaumont
had two levels containing barrack accommodation for 1,000 men
and the necessary amenities including a water reservoir, kitchens,
ammunition magazines, armoury, storerooms and an infirmary. All
this was protected by a concrete roof more than three metres thick
containing an integral metre-deep layer of sand designed to act as
a shock absorber. The concrete was buried under a further four
metres of earth for additional protection.[6] The fort's main armament
consisted of two heavily armoured, retractable cupolas operated by
forty-eight-ton counterweights. One mounted a short-barrelled
155mm gun and the other two 75mm pieces. Fire from these guns
was controlled from four armoured observation domes, which were
in turn protected by three retractable machine gun turrets. Additional
75mm guns and smaller calibre, quick-firing pieces were mounted
in more conventional emplacements covering the rear and western
side of the fort called the Casemate de Bourges, while the barracks
themselves were provided with loopholes for rearward defence.[7] The
only apparent weakness was the lack of an extended tunnel access
to the fort's south-facing entrance, which exposed anyone entering
or leaving the fort to hostile artillery fire.

Thus by 1914 Verdun's defences were formidable, but as in 1792 things were not quite what they seemed. French analysis of the events of 1870–71 drew the not unreasonable conclusion that a lack of offensive spirit had played a key role in their poor performance. Unfortunately, the perceived solution was a swing to the opposite extreme that elevated the offensive above all other military actions and vested it with near mystic qualities. Among the most influential propagators of this doctrine was Colonel Loyzeau de Grandmaison, head of the Troisième Bureau of the Grand Quartier Général (GQG), who set his ideas down on paper in 1906.[8] By 1911 de Grandmaison had refined his doctrine into a series of lectures which were used as the basis for the official training and operational manuals used by the French Army in 1914. According to de Grandmaison, enemy intentions and actions were irrelevant. Victory merely required knowing where the enemy was, unambiguous orders for attack, and for the assault to be delivered with sufficient audacity, violence and will, even in the face of superior numbers. Tactics were rendered down to manoeuvring troops to within fifty metres of the enemy, from where they could launch an irresistible bayonet charge that would overwhelm the enemy before they could bring their fire to bear. Everything was subordinated to this aim, with artillery participation being restricted to supporting rather than preparatory fire, for example, and similar constraints being placed upon the cavalry and other supporting arms. To this end the artillery was equipped largely with the light, fast-firing 75mm field gun, known colloquially as the *soixante-quinze*, in lieu of anything heavier.[9]

By the time the French Army went to war in 1914 this doctrine of offensive *à l'outrance* (roughly 'attack to the extremes'), fuelled by a near-mystical reliance on élan vital, had completely permeated the Army. It was promoted and articulated at the top by future marshals including Foch and de Castelnau, who lectured enthusiastically on the subject at the École de Guerre. At the bottom, fresh conscripts were indoctrinated with it from the moment they reported for service. In 1913 Charles de Gaulle, recently graduated from the French military academy at Saint-Cyr, greeted a group of recruits with a speech informing them that the act of advancing on the enemy with the bayonet was the primary concern of general and private alike.[10] To reinforce the point, all recruits were obliged to learn a catechism extolling closing with the bayonet as the ultimate military virtue.[11]

By harking back to the military glories of the First Empire, the doctrine of offensive *à l'outrance* restored the Army's badly dented self-confidence, its standing in wider society, and did the same for France as a whole. Even the political left, which had no love for the Army after its ruthless crushing of the Paris Commune in 1871, saw it as a return to the 1792 levée en masse that safeguarded the Revolution. The wrangling over the adoption of a less visible uniform for the Army in the run-up to 1914 illustrates the extent to which de Grandmaison's ideas had become accepted in French civilian society. Advances in battlefield firepower led the British to adopt a low-visibility khaki uniform in 1902, and the Germans followed suit with a feldgrau field uniform in 1910. The French Army trialled blue-grey and beige-grey uniforms in 1902 and 1903, which were rejected as being too similar to German equivalents, and a grey-green outfit was rejected in 1911 for being too similar to contemporary Italian outfits. However, these rejections were politically motivated rather than based on practical or tactical considerations. The French political right saw any attempt to replace the existing dark blue greatcoat and red trousers as a plot by the left to reduce the Army to a citizen militia, particularly in the wake of the Dreyfus Affair in 1899. Red trousers thus came to be viewed as a vital element in the promotion and maintenance of national and military élan. The *Echo de Paris* denounced camouflage uniforms as a Masonic plot, and in 1913 Minister of War Eugène Etienne insisted that 'Red trousers are France'. The fact that the garment had only been adopted in 1829 to support the French madder dye industry was conveniently overlooked among the rhetoric. The end result was that the French Army went to war in 1914 in the same

2 Verdun before 1914, looking north across the Meuse. The twin towers of Verdun Cathedral are visible on the skyline.

uniform as it had in 1870, for although a drab *horizon-bleu* uniform was adopted before the outbreak of hostilities, it did not go into production until August 1914.[12]

Although potentially hazardous from a career perspective, there was some dissent to the prevailing orthodoxy. General Pierre Ruffey warned that near total reliance on the excellent *soixante-quinze* field gun was unwise,[13] and Colonel Philippe Pétain preached the simple dictum that firepower killed and would therefore have an unwelcome and lethal effect on attackers, irrespective of their ardour and élan.[14] Pétain's point was rendered especially pertinent by the doctrinal insistence that all French soil was to be defended to the death without exception, and that any territory captured by the enemy had to be regained by immediate counter-attack on pain of court martial. General Charles Lanrezac was therefore justified in pointing out that untrammelled offensive action would make it virtually impossible for corps commanders and above to impose any meaningful control over their subordinate formations. Furthermore, the rigid doctrine of immediate counter-attack removed any latitude for individual initiative.[15]

Dissent of this kind was very much in the minority, however, and support for the cult of the offensive extended virtually unchallenged to the very top of the Army hierarchy. Thus Marshal Joseph Joffre's introduction to the French Army's strategic plan for war with Germany proclaimed that 'whatever the circumstances, it is the Commander-in-Chief's intention to advance with all forces united to attack the German armies'.[16] Plan XVII was a combined mobilisation framework and plan for offensive action to regain the lost provinces of Alsace and Lorraine, employing four of the five French field armies totalling 800,000 men. It was to open with a rapid spoiling offensive into Alsace while the French Army was still mobilising, designed to unbalance German mobilisation and channel any riposte into the Belfort Gap. This would be followed up with a larger attack after mobilisation was complete, oriented just north of Metz, intended to destroy the German centre and to stymie any attempt to outflank the French fixed defences by cutting across neutral Belgian territory. This would in turn permit a general eastward advance that would re-establish the Franco-German border on the Rhine.[17]

2

Setting the Scene: August 1914–February 1915

War broke out at the beginning of August 1914, and initially things went well for the French. Unlike in 1870, mobilisation went like clockwork and compliance outstripped official expectations. The Army anticipated a shortfall of up to thirteen per cent, whereas only one and a half per cent, equivalent to 1,600 men, failed to report as ordered and many of these were vagrants or mentally unfit.[18] Around 4,300 trains carried 1,500,000 men forward to railheads in the ten-day period beginning 1 August 1914, from where they marched to their concentration areas at a rate of up to thirty kilometres a day.[19] General Bonneau's 7th Corps, from the French 1st Army, launched the initial advance into Alsace on 7 August. The first troops across the frontier tore up the German marker posts and sent them to be laid on the grave of the extreme nationalist and patriotic poet Paul Déroulêde before triumphing in their first clash with the Germans at Altkirch. The six-hour battle was decided by a bayonet charge as per the regulations, and the victors moved on to occupy the city of Mulhouse the following day, on 8 August.

Thereafter, however, things began to go awry. 7th Corps was driven back out of Mulhouse on 9 August and Bonneau, worried by a lack of reinforcement and reports of large German forces moving to cut him off, retired to the safety of Belfort where he was promptly relieved of his command. The main French attack into Alsace, spearheaded by the 1st and 2nd Armies advancing north and east toward Sarrebourg and Morhange respectively, crossed the frontier with bands playing on 15 August. After a five-day advance that attained both objectives and reoccupied Mulhouse the two French armies lost contact in the broken terrain. Both were then struck by a series of German counter-attacks that pushed them south-west back into French territory, occupied St-Dié and Lunéville on 23 August and threatened Nancy; Mulhouse was evacuated for the last time four days later. The second part of Plan XVII, the advance on Metz and Neufchâteau in the Ardennes by the French 3rd and 4th Armies, was launched on 22 August and fared no better. Both formations were stopped cold by overwhelming German machine gun and artillery fire in spite of repeated, near suicidal bayonet charges led by white-gloved officers. Pétain's pre-war warnings proved terribly prescient.[20] The two-week Battle of the Frontiers cost the French Army 300,000 casualties including 4,778 officers, the latter representing 10 per cent of the Army's entire officer strength.[21]

The French assumed that German operations along the Franco-German border were their main effort, and they were also expecting a limited trespass through neutral Luxembourg and the Belgian Ardennes to outflank the northern end of the Séré de Rivières line. Joffre had strenuously advocated doing the same in 1912, but the idea was rejected by a French government mindful of the diplomatic repercussions.[22] The Germans laboured under no such inhibitions, however, and their premeditated violation of neutral Belgian territory went much further than the French imagined. Faced with the prospect of a two-front war the German General Staff came up with the Schlieffen Plan, which advocated a holding action against the Russians in the east whilst the bulk of the German Army, some 700,000 men, inflicted a swift defeat on the French in the west. This was to be achieved via an advance into central Belgium at Liège, which would then carry out a huge wheeling movement that would pass west of Paris, besiege the city and continue east to annihilate the French armies facing Alsace and Lorraine in a final, climactic battle.

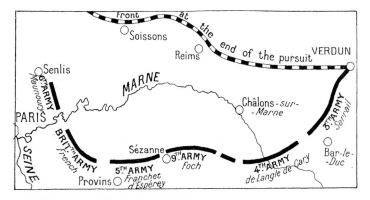

3 Verdun – pivot of the Battle of the Marne.

The impetuous French attacks along the Franco-German border demanded by Plan XVII thus played straight into German hands.

Whether the Schlieffen Plan was feasible using just muscle power is open to debate, but in the event a series of seemingly unconnected circumstances conspired to derail it. The Russians moved faster than expected and launched an attack into East Prussia before their mobilisation was complete, which obliged the Germans to redirect units en route to Belgium to the east as reinforcements. Neither did the advance into Belgium proceed as scheduled. The German attack on the forts protecting Liège began on 5 August 1914, using home-grown 420mm guns and 305mm howitzers borrowed from their Austro-Hungarian allies. However, it was nine days before German columns could move through the area unimpeded and the last fort did not fall until two days after that, on 16 August. Most seriously of all, the German commanders on the ground, believing they faced negligible opposition at best, redirected the wheeling movement east of Paris. This opened their right flank to a newly formed French army in the French capital, some of whom travelled to battle in the famous 'Taxis of the Marne'. The German Army was fought to a standstill along a line looping south from Paris to Verdun between 6 and 9 September 1914, with the latter serving as the eastern anchor of the Allied line. The subsequent German withdrawal in the west prompted the so-called 'Race to the Sea', a series of outflanking moves that continued north until the Belgian coast and mutual exhaustion brought operations to an end. By the end of 1914 combined German casualties totalled around 750,000 and the French had lost 300,000 dead and 600,000 wounded, missing and captured.[23] At least some of the latter continued the fight after they could reasonably have been expected to desist. After being cut off in Lorraine in August a 300-strong party under a Captain de Colbert waged a guerrilla campaign against the Germans that lasted until the last were captured or killed in December.[24]

The fighting front of the first five months of mobile operations thus stabilised into a continuous line running from the Swiss border to the English Channel, along which the Germans had selected the most advantageous terrain features. They occupied the small folds that pass for high ground east of Ypres, the Messines Ridge, the mining spoil heaps and steep ridges running south toward Arras, and the rolling chalk crests straddling the River Somme. They burrowed into the Chemin des Dames (Ladies' Way) ridge overlooking the River Aisne, fortified crests in the Champagne, hilltops in the Argonne and Meuse Heights and mountaintops in the Vosges, where the French staked a claim to a small corner of Germany proper. Thus securely ensconced the Germans were content to sit back and let the Allies come to them through the second year of the war. The exceptions were a limited German attack near Ypres on 22 April 1915 that employed 500 cylinders of chlorine gas, the first large-scale use of chemical weapons, and a more conventional assault on the Meuse in June.

The French launched their first major offensive on 16 February 1915 in Champagne, east of Reims; it petered out on 18 March after an advance of three kilometres that cost 40,000 casualties. Attention then shifted north to Picardy and Artois. The British lost over 11,000 men at Neuve-Chapelle in March 1915, another 11,000 at Aubers Ridge in May and 61,000 including over 7,000 dead at Loos in September, for minimal territorial gain. French operations on the British right flank in Artois cost them over 16,000 dead, nearly 80,000 wounded and a further 20,000 missing. The remains of 40,000 of them are still there, interred in the French National Memorial cemetery atop the Notre Dame de Lorette ridge north of Arras. The final French attack in Artois coincided with a renewed effort in Champagne, beginning on 25 September 1915. The latter started well, piercing the German first line and taking 14,000 prisoners, but the French were unable to maintain their momentum

4 The Vauban ramparts protecting the western side of Verdun's Citadel. The ornate gateway with the sentries in the right foreground is the Neuve Porte leading to the main entrance to the underground portion of the Citadel, 200 metres or so to the right on the Rue de Rû.

5 The Underground Citadel had four kilometres of passageways and could provide food and accommodation for 6,000 men. This casemate has been pressed into service as a barrack room. Note the vaulted brick roof, electric lighting and ceramic insulators on the power cable in the upper right. Contemporary accounts suggest that accommodation was much more crowded and the atmosphere much less clear and wholesome, which might explain the rather unnatural stiffness of the 'relaxing' soldiery.

6 A soldiers' canteen in the Underground Citadel. Note the amount and variety of wine on offer behind the counter. The provision of pinard, as the ration wine was called, was considered a key factor in maintaining morale. The ration was increased from a quarter to half a litre per man per day during the war, and a spirit called *gniole* was issued to troops in inclement weather conditions, in the same way the British Army issued GS rum.

7 The Verdun sector before the German offensive of February 1916. Note the location of the forts and their fields of fire.

through a German defence zone up to five kilometres deep. The Champagne offensive was called off on 6 October, that in Artois five days later, for a combined cost of 30,000 dead and 160,000 wounded and missing; this elevated French total casualties by the end of 1915 to 1.2 million, including 350,000 killed or missing.[25]

The exception to all this was Verdun, where the most defensible terrain was already occupied by French fortifications. There the front line bulged north and east into German-held territory on the east bank of the Meuse, before swinging south toward the foothills of the Vosges. Fire from the outlying forts east of the Meuse prevented the Germans from outflanking General Maurice Sarrail's 3rd Army as it retired from its abortive advance toward Metz and reoriented north to face the German advance into the Argonne. The Germans treated the works close to Verdun with respect but launched a concerted effort to cut the town off in September 1914. This came close to success, and not merely because the German advances south through the Argonne and west on the Meuse Heights came within seven miles of each other on 10 September.[26] Joffre, considering the town doomed and remembering how the French field armies had bottled themselves up at Metz and Sedan in 1870, ordered Verdun abandoned. Sarrail, the man on the spot, did not share Joffre's opinion and chose to ignore the order. In so doing he arguably saved the French from losing the war. Without Verdun as a lynchpin it is doubtful that the Battle of the Marne could have been fought, and

8 The last train from Verdun, wrecked by German shellfire near the Côte du Poivre, six kilometres north of the town. Note the abandoned artillery limber in the foreground, possibly from a French 75mm gun battery.

there would have been little to stop the German armies in Alsace and Lorraine sweeping on to Paris and beyond.[27]

Be that as it may, the German advance from the east involved tackling some of the outlying French defence works. Fort Troyon, on the east bank of the Meuse fifteen miles south of Verdun, was besieged on 8 September 1914 and, although relieved by a French counter-attack on 13 September, was reduced to untenable rubble by a five-day bombardment. The Germans renewed their attack on 22 September with an assault on Fort Camp des Romains at St Mihiel, midway between Verdun and Toul. The fort fell on 26 September after *Infanterie Régiment* 11 overran part of its ramparts and penetrated its underground galleries. This allowed the Germans to cross the Meuse, occupy the village of Chauvoncourt and cut one of the mainline railways running into Verdun. The other, which ran west to Châlons-en-Champagne, was within sight of German artillery observers where it passed through the Argonne. The last train on the line running north along the west bank of the Meuse was destroyed by shelling just north of the town, where the Côte du Poivre creates a loop in the river. Verdun was thus left reliant upon a narrow-gauge military railway and road running to Bar-le-Duc, thirty miles to the south-west.[28]

3

Framing the Battlefield: February 1915– February 1916

The German attacks of September 1914 also seized two locations that were to be the major focus of fighting in the region the following year. The Les Éparges ridge, fifteen miles south-east of Verdun, was occupied on 21 September 1914 because it provided a commanding view north-west toward Verdun, and thus formed the southern shoulder of the salient around the town. Around a mile in length and 1000 feet high, the ridge climbs eastward from the village of the Les Éparges, with an intermediate peak roughly midway along its length, dubbed 'Point C'. It then rises to the high point at 'Point X', where it drops away abruptly to the Woëvre Plain. Once in possession the Germans transformed the feature into a fortress, with five successive defence lines ascending the ridge and protecting Point C, although the French established a presence on the western slopes through a series of limited attacks that ended on 16 October 1914. In January 1915 GQG decided that the German-held portion of the ridge would provide a good base from which to eliminate the German foothold across the Meuse at St Mihiel to the south. The French 13th and 106th *Régiments d'Infanterie* (RI) were thus detailed to take the ridge and Army engineers were instructed to tunnel into the ridge to position explosive charges under the German positions, using information gleaned from German prisoners.

The attack began at 14.00 on 17 February 1915 with the detonation of four mines under the German front line, after which the 106th RI moved forward to seize what remained of the German trenches and the 100-foot-deep craters created by the mines. This was achieved by the late evening but further advance was prevented by fierce

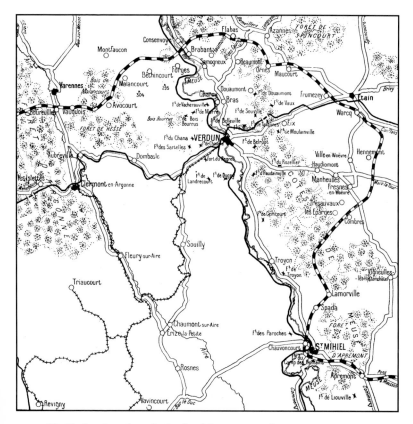

9 The Verdun front from the Battle of the Marne to the great German offensive in 1916. Note the flanking heights of Les Éparges to the south-east and Vauquois to the north-west.

German counter-attacks. Although the attack failed to reach Point C as planned, the 106th Infantry held onto their gains but at a heavy cost; the regiment lost 300 dead, 1,000 wounded and a further 300 missing in the three days up to 19 February. Further French attacks on 18, 19 and 27 March were rebuffed, with the Germans exploding counter-mines containing twenty to thirty tonnes of explosive apiece. The western end of the ridge including Point C finally fell to the French after three full-scale attacks over the five day period ending on 9 April 1915, and once again the units involved suffered heavily in the attack and from the subsequent German ripostes. By 10 April the 25th Battaillon de Chasseurs à Pied (BCP), the light infantry unit that finally seized Point C, had lost 474 men, and a casualty count by the 67th RI two days later recorded 1,029 killed, wounded and missing.[29] In the event, Point X remained in German hands until September 1918. By that time the topography of the ridge had been permanently altered by a score of huge craters along the crest and slopes.

Events unfolded in a similar fashion at the opposite shoulder of the Verdun salient, fifteen miles west of the town. Standing 295 metres above sea level, the Butte de Vauquois was topped by a small village of the same name. The 168 inhabitants were evacuated on the night of 3/4 September 1914, and the hilltop was occupied by troops from the French 9th *Division d'Infanterie* (DI) on 15 September. After a sharp German artillery barrage the latter were driven off the Butte on 24 September by *Infanterie Division* 33, losing fifty dead and 150 wounded in the process. Recognising the value of the hill as an observation point over the French lines as far as the railway linking Verdun with Châlons-en-Champagne, the Germans set about fortifying the hill with their customary efficiency. Limited French attacks to regain the feature began in October 1914 but achieved little apart from closing up to the southern base of the hill. A sustained attack by the 10th DI between 17 February and 4 March 1915 finally succeeded in reaching the hilltop and securing the southern half of the village. The final stage of the attack, between 28 February and 4 March, cost some 3,000 French dead and missing, and ended with the front lines occupying the ruined buildings lining the village's central main street. Thereafter both sides fell back on mine warfare as a means of breaking the stalemate and driving their opponents off the hilltop.

Mine warfare actually began at Vauquois before the stalemate. The Germans deployed Pionier Bataillon 30 to the hill on 7 January 1915, and the French detonated their first charge on 3 February 1915. Thereafter the size and depth of the mines escalated to the extent that the Butte de Vauquois became 'the most heavily-mined spot on the earth's surface'.[30] In March 1915 the average charge was in the range of five to 1,500 kilograms and was five to fifteen metres deep; within a year charges had grown to an average of fifteen tonnes buried at depths of up to forty metres. The Germans exploded a 4.7-tonne mine on 3 March 1916 and on 25 March the French replied with a 12-tonne charge that totally demolished Vauquois church. The largest mine, containing sixty tonnes of explosive, was detonated by the Germans on 14 May 1916. The explosion killed 108 French soldiers from the 46th RI and an attached engineer unit and blew out the whole western end of the hill, creating a crater 250 feet wide and sixty feet deep.

In all, in excess of 500 separate charges were detonated in the Butte de Vauquois, either mines intended to destroy positions on the surface or smaller camouflet charges designed to collapse enemy tunnels and workings. The hill was honeycombed with seventeen kilometres of tunnels on three levels, with chambers to house barracks, stores, infirmaries, electrical generators and compressors to channel air to the deepest tunnels. On the surface a German mine destroyed the village well and the last surviving chestnut tree on the hilltop on 24 February 1917. These were the last visible signs of human habitation on the hilltop, which had been reduced to a string of huge, interlinked craters up to eighty metres wide and ten to twenty metres deep. The front-line trenches ran along the rims of the craters, in places incorporating the foundations of vanished buildings. The two final charges were a French mine detonated in March 1918, followed by a German camouflet on 9 April. The latter withdrew five days later, and the Butte de Vauquois was liberated without a fight by troops from the US 35th Infantry Division on 26 September 1918, almost exactly four years after it was occupied by the Germans.

While all this was going on Verdun remained an island of relative calm. In February 1915 German aircraft bombed the town,[31] no doubt assisting in the ongoing reduction of the town's civilian population, which by the beginning of 1916 had dropped from 15,000 to 3,000.[32] In the same month the Germans brought up a battery of 420mm guns to try their hand at Forts Douaumont and Vaux. Sixty-two rounds were fired, creating a huge plume of

10 Smoke rising from fires in Verdun. The town first came under fire from German aircraft in February 1915.

dust and smoke which in conjunction with the lack of return fire
misled the German observers into assuming they had inflicted lethal
damage. In fact the damage, while visually impressive, was largely
superficial. The eastern end of Douaumont's external barracks collapsed into the courtyard and part of the inscription over the main
entrance was blown away, but the protected portion of the fort was
unaffected apart from a severe shaking from the concussion of the
huge rounds. Most importantly, all the fort's retractable gun cupolas
remained operational. The reason for the lack of French return fire
was simple; Douaumont's short-barrelled 155mm piece lacked the
range to reach the German front line, let alone the gun emplacements some distance behind it.[33]

11 Fort Douaumont after bombardment by German 420mm 'Big Bertha'
howitzers in February 1915. The German guns fired sixty-two rounds at the
fort, collapsing part of its external barracks into the courtyard. While visually
spectacular, this had no effect on the fort's armament or defensive integrity,
and inflicted no casualties.

12 The damage
inflicted on Fort
Douaumont's
main entrance
in February
1915. Note the
damage to the
fort's name
inscribed over
the gateway.

However, Douaumont's resilience under shellfire availed it little against a more insidious threat. As we have seen, there was little room in the offensive *à l'outrance* doctrine for fixed defences; the Army's operational manuals decreed that the only legitimate purpose for fortresses and fixed defences was to allow manpower to be freed up for the attack elsewhere. In the official French view the fact that Douaumont had shrugged off hits from the largest guns the enemy could muster, or that the Belgian defences at Liège had inflicted a critical nine-day delay on the German advance, counted for little. The crucial point was that the forts at Liège had fallen, and their obsolescence was dismissed by pointing to the failure of Fort Manonviller, one of the largest and most modern French works located near Lunéville at the southern end of the Séré de Rivières line. Manonviller was evacuated on 23 August 1914, after the fumes created by 1,500 German shells of up to 420mm calibre rendered it untenable.[34] Joffre's misplaced order for Verdun to be abandoned in September 1914 showed that the outbreak of hostilities had not changed the official view of fixed fortifications. This still tallied with General Auguste-Alexandre Ducrot's opinion on being encircled in Sedan in 1870: '*Nous sommes dans un pot de chambre, et nous y serons emmerdés*' (we are in a chamber pot and we are going to be shat upon).[35] Joffre and GQG had no intention of allowing such an occurrence to happen again.

The one useful purpose of fixed fortifications acknowledged by the latter was as a source of artillery for redeployment elsewhere. To make this process easier the status of the works around Verdun was steadily degraded through 1915. Previously independent commands, all the forts were regrouped into an overall Région Fortifiée under a General Coutanceau, who was in turn subordinate to the regional front commander. Where the power lay in this relationship became clear in July 1915 when Coutanceau contradicted General Auguste Dubail, Commander Eastern Group of Armies, in his insistence that GQG's artillery stripping policy was correct. Coutanceau was promptly sacked and replaced in August by another general named Herr. Dubail left Herr in no doubt that the gun stripping policy came directly from the top and that fixed defences had no legitimate role in modern warfare. He was also expressly forbidden to fight for Verdun or to become invested there, and ordered to prepare defences west of the Meuse in case it became necessary to withdraw from the town. By the end of October 1915 sufficient guns to equip the equivalent of fifty-four artillery batteries and 128,000 rounds of ammunition had been stripped from the forts and ouvrages around Verdun. Fort Douaumont was reduced to the single 155mm and two

75mm pieces built inextricably into its retractable cupolas, and plans were afoot to remove these too.[36]

The weakening of Verdun's defences was exacerbated by complacency among the French troops manning the trenches in the Verdun sector. Initially, the events of 1914 had prompted the construction of a belt of trenches linking and protecting the forts and ouvrages up to three miles deep in places.[37] By June 1915 this urgency had evaporated, however, and troops exhausted from the fighting elsewhere on the front were being posted to the Verdun sector to rest. These men were understandably reluctant to expend their energy in digging or needlessly provoking their opponents, and a live-and-let-live mentality developed on both sides of the line as a result. French participant accounts refer to a schedule of four days in the front line followed by four days in reserve, with little interrupting interminable card games. One French officer was forced to issue a stern warning to his men about the perils of communicating or even fraternising with the enemy.[38]

Had the Germans facing Verdun remained quiescent, or had the German policymakers maintained their defensive stance, this might not have been a problem. However, the failure of the Schlieffen Plan led to the Chief of the German General Staff, Field Marshal Helmuth von Moltke, being replaced by Erich von Falkenhayn on 14 September 1914. Events in 1915 convinced Falkenhayn that the war had to be decided in the west, which formed the gist of a memorandum assessing the strategic situation prepared for Kaiser Wilhelm II and delivered at the beginning of December 1915. The memo identified Britain as the major threat and, via some rather convoluted logic, concluded that the most effective counter to the major threat would be to knock France out of the war. The best way to achieve this was via an assault on Belfort or Verdun, prestige targets that would oblige a strong French reaction, with Verdun being the preferred option. Falkenhayn visited the Kaiser at Potsdam in the middle of December to expand on his ideas, which give every impression of being deliberately packaged to pander to the Kaiser's prejudices and preferences. Wilhelm apparently held Britain responsible for the death of his father and for denying Germany her rightful imperial 'place in the sun', among other things, and his son Crown Prince Wilhelm commanded the German 5th Army that had been facing Verdun since the end of 1914. Be that as it may, Falkenhayn left Potsdam with his ideas approved, under the code name 'Gericht'.[39]

Operation Gericht was not a straightforward attack to take Verdun, however. Instead, it envisaged merely threatening the town with a series of limited attacks. The underlying purpose of this tactic was, in Falkenhayn's own words, to provoke the French Army 'to throw in every man they have. If they do so the forces of France will bleed to death…'[40] He was thus bluntly proposing Ermattungsstrategie, a deliberate battle of attrition and, possibly for the first time in modern warfare, was thus advocating directly trading his own soldiers' lives for those of the enemy as a military objective in its own right, on the assumption that he could afford to sacrifice more lives than they could. Even the title of the operation pointed to its macabre intent, for while *Gericht* can be translated as 'tribunal' or 'judgement', it can also mean 'execution place'.[41] If the French took the bait as intended there was every prospect of Verdun falling as a result, and the objective of bleeding the French Army white could be achieved whether the town fell or not. Gericht thus offered the attractive prospect of a no-lose strategy for the Germans.

Recent work has cast doubt on whether Falkenhayn really did propose a deliberate battle of attrition, and suggests that he was merely reflecting a general military tendency that influenced his British and French opposite numbers.[42] However, his behaviour, and especially his dealings with commanders tasked to carry out the operation, strongly suggest not only that was this the case but that Falkenhayn was also well aware that the attrition would not be the one-way process implied by his memorandum. Neither the Crown Prince nor his Chief of Staff, General Schmidt von Knobelsdorf, appear to have seen the memo, even though Falkenhayn actually informed von Knobelsdorf that an attack towards Verdun had been approved in person immediately after his meeting with the Kaiser. They were thus unaware of the memorandum's content or the underlying intent of Gericht, and Falkenhayn ensured they remained unenlightened. The Crown Prince and Knobelsdorf advocated attacking Verdun with a simultaneous advance along both banks of the Meuse, but Falkenhayn refused to allocate them sufficient troops claiming the need to maintain a large reserve to counter the expected Allied response, especially from the British. However, this possibility was refuted by the Chief of Staff of the German 6th Army facing the British, who pointed out that their New Army was far from combat ready. His superior, Crown Prince Rupprecht of Bavaria, went on the record saying that Falkenhayn's intent was unclear and contradictory.

However, when taken in context with his December memorandum, the motivation behind Falkenhayn's behaviour toward the 5th Army is quite clear. An advance of the strength advocated by Crown Prince Wilhelm and von Knobelsdorf down both banks of the Meuse might well take Verdun in short order, and would thus remove the opportunity to bleed the French Army to death. A weaker attack was therefore imperative to draw the French into reinforcing their line, and Falkenhayn's limitation on the size of the initial attack force and subsequent tardiness in supplying reinforcements guaranteed that this was how matters unfolded. It also explains why Falkenhayn was careful to conceal the reality of Gericht. Troops aware of the fact they were being cynically deployed as mere bait were unlikely to perform satisfactorily, and the fiction of a full-scale attack to capture Verdun was vital to safeguard German morale. Falkenhayn was therefore obliged to hide the truth from his soldiers, and it is thus difficult to disagree with Alistair Horne's judgement that 'seldom in the history of war can the commander of a great army have been so cynically deceived as was the German Crown Prince by Falkenhayn'.[43]

Be that as it may, German preparations for Gericht were impressive in both speed and scale. Between 24 December 1915 and 12 February 1916, when the attack was to begin, 140,000 troops were moved up to the eight-mile frontage running east from the Meuse selected for the attack. They joined a similar number already in place, with whole villages of French civilians being evicted to make room and remove prying eyes from behind the Meuse Heights. Ten new railway lines with two dozen stations were constructed, along with miles of narrow-gauge track to carry men, munitions and materiel almost up to the front line. The latter moved a million sandbags, 125,000 hand grenades, 17,000 digging tools and 6,000 wire cutters for one German formation alone. Large concrete shelters called Stollen, some capable of holding 1,000 men, were constructed up to a kilometre behind the front line to conceal the assault troops and prevent the French detecting their presence in the front-line trenches.

The greatest effort, however, was dedicated to the artillery. By 1 February 1916 the 5th Army's artillery units had lost thirty per cent of their horses moving in excess of 1,200 guns into position facing the Verdun salient, and 1,300 trains brought in 2,750,000 shells, some containing gas, sufficient to feed the guns for six days' intensive firing. In part this reflected German artillery practice which, unlike the developing British preference for long artillery preparation, favoured comparatively short but extremely heavy shelling imme-diately before attacks began; thus the nine-hour bombardment that was to open Operation Gericht was the heaviest in history to that date. More importantly, artillery was the instrument Falkenhayn had chosen to inflict his bleeding treatment on the French Army, and the various German guns were thus woven into a sophisticated fire plan than reached well behind the front line.

The overall aim was clearly laid out in the German artillery orders: 'No line is to remain unbombarded, no possibilities of supply unmolested, nowhere should the enemy feel safe.' Thus Minenwerfer bomb-throwers of various calibres, 77mm field pieces and 210mm guns were tasked to obliterate the French front line, with a full battery of the latter being targeted on all 150 yards of it. 130mm pieces were to probe the French support trenches and positions. 150mm guns were assigned to wipe out known French artillery positions with a mixture of explosives and gas, to stifle any new batteries the French might bring up, and to shell all the roads and tracks linking the French front line to their rear areas. Thirteen 420mm and seventeen 305mm howitzers were to pound the French forts, and three 380mm naval guns were tasked to interdict the bridges in Verdun proper and road and rail links miles behind the town. Gun pits were dug at night, painstakingly camouflaged and stocked with ammunition before the guns were actually installed. Preparation for the three 380mm naval pieces deployed in the Bois de Warphémont, Bois de Muzeray and Bois de Spincourt seventeen miles north-east of Verdun were even more sophisticated. These guns were mounted on traversable platforms rooted in huge concrete emplacements that incorporated their sophisticated fire control equipment, with concrete-protected underground ammunition stores linked to the gun platforms by light railway, and closely resembled the installations erected on the Atlantic Wall twenty-five years later. Ranging shots were staggered to make them look like random harassing fire, and in the later stages only guns assumed to be known to the French were used for routine fire tasks.

The Germans went to great lengths to conceal their activities. French civilians were forcibly removed from the area behind the German lines, and men were employed manufacturing and painting huge amounts of camouflage netting. Additional aircraft and anti-aircraft guns were drafted in to deny French reconnaissance aircraft access to German airspace, which they succeeded in doing almost until the last minute; once Gericht was launched they were to revert to protecting their own artillery observation balloons. Neither was the German concealment effort restricted to the Verdun area. Internal security was tight. Liaison officers from elsewhere were banned from the 5th Army's area, and the details of the artillery fire plan were even kept from Falkenhayn's chief artillery officer. Units to the south were encouraged to plan and prepare for an attack on Belfort as a disinformation measure, an illusion reinforced by a well-publicised visit from Crown Prince Wilhelm. Artillery programmes were carried out on other sectors of the front to create the impression of impending attack, and German agents in neutral countries spread rumours that any operations near Verdun were merely a diversion.

The German security and disinformation effort was aided and abetted by a combination of happenstance, geography and climate. French intelligence was hobbled by the loss of one of their major spy networks operating behind the German lines just before preparations for Gericht began. The broken, wooded terrain and foggy winter weather handicapped ground reconnaissance, and the French troops on the spot were less than diligent. They carried out little if any patrolling, French front-line units preferring to rely on the less uncomfortable and dangerous but also substantially less reliable listening posts. All of this exacerbated the general air of complacency that had grown up at Verdun from mid-1915, although many commanders did what they could to counteract it and draw attention to the weakness of Verdun's defences generally. These included the commander of the *Région Fortifiée du Verdun* General Herr, who badgered GQG for reinforcements constantly, citing his instruction to prepare defences west of Verdun as justification, but to no avail.

Another especially notable boat-rocker was Lieutenant-Colonel Émile Driant, sixty-year-old commander of the 56th and 59th BCP holding the front line in the Bois de Caures, eight miles north of Verdun. In July 1915, concerned that he had insufficient men to man the front line or the materiel and equipment to carry out ordered improvements to his positions, Driant appealed to his immediate superior. When this failed to elicit a satisfactory response he passed his concerns and growing suspicion that the Germans were preparing a major attack in the region to the President of the Chamber of Deputies in Paris, Paul Deschanel, at the end of August 1915. Driant had been Deputy for Nancy before the war and Deschanel was a personal friend. Deschanel duly passed them to Minister of War Joseph Galliéni, who promptly despatched a delegation to Verdun to investigate. When this confirmed Driant's concerns he passed their report to Joffre with a request for an explanation. This did not go down at all well, and Horne is probably correct in his view that had events not intervened, Driant would have been court-martialled.[44]

Be that as it may, it was impossible to totally conceal preparations of the magnitude of Gericht, and by January 1916 the signs were becoming increasingly obvious. At the beginning of the month German artillery ranging shots were noted along with the disappearance of church spires behind the latter's lines; these provided ranging markers for French counter-battery fire. Rumours of large-scale German troop movements were supported by information from German deserters about large dumps of artillery ammunition including gas shells, and about the Stollen constructed just behind the German front line. It was the latter information that finally gained Herr some attention. On 24 January 1916 General Édouard de Castelnau, Joffre's chief-of-staff, arrived in Verdun for an inspection. When this confirmed Herr's assessment, de Castelnau rescinded the order for new defences west of Verdun, ordered Herr to concentrate on strengthening the existing first and second lines east of the Meuse and promised him reinforcements. The 51st and 72nd DIs, formed from reservists from Lille and Lorraine respectively, arrived on 12 February 1916 and the 7th and 30th Corps arrived shortly afterward.

This was too little, too late, however, for the French had run out of time. Gericht was scheduled to begin on 12 February, but was postponed due to bad weather, with fog and snow making artillery observation impossible. Possibly due to information from German deserters, the French front-line troops stood to through the nights of 11/12 and 12/13 February, which did not go down well when the expected attack failed to materialise. The German assault troops were obliged to spend over a week in their Stollen, subsisting on canned rations and frequently in several inches of water as the shelters were not designed for more than short-term and temporary occupation. The weather cleared on 20 February and the Germans put down a bombardment in the afternoon, which may have been to finish their ranging programme. Whichever, the night of 20–21 February was quiet, cold and clear, so much so that the French could hear the German supply trains and the sound of singing from the German trenches.[45]

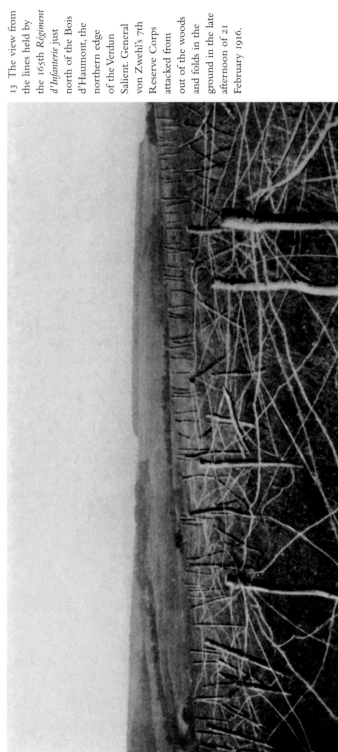

13 The view from the lines held by the 165th *Régiment d'Infanterie* just north of the Bois d'Haumont, the northern edge of the Verdun Salient. General von Zwehl's 7th Reserve Corps attacked from out of the woods and folds in the ground in the late afternoon of 21 February 1916.

4

The Battle Begins:
21–28 February 1916

The first shots of Operation Gericht appear to have been fired by the 380mm Krupp naval guns sited in the Bois de Warphémont, at 04.00 on 21 February 1916. According to legend, the first round was aimed at the Meuse bridges in the town but actually landed in the cathedral yard. Others landed more accurately and reduced the rail yard to a cratered ruin in short order.[46] The full bombardment began at or just after 07.00 French time across the entire Verdun salient, and its concussion was noticeable 150 miles away in the Vosges Mountains.[47] Shells rained down at a rate of forty a minute for hour after hour, obliterating French positions, cutting telephone lines, uprooting trees and demolishing dug-outs and concrete bunkers, killing or burying those sheltering within as the curtain of fire worked its way remorselessly back and forth. French artillery positions were saturated with high explosive and phosgene gas shells, against which French respirators offered no protection, and counter-fire fell away to almost nothing. French long-range guns did, however, manage to blow up a German regimental paymaster with his cash box, at Billy-sur-Mangiennes, near the Bois de Warphémont, and another French salvo straddled the 5th Army forward HQ at Vittarville just as von Knobelsdorf was reporting to the Crown Prince. The Crown Prince and his entourage hastily withdrew to their permanent HQ at Stenay, fifteen miles further north.[48]

At around midday the barrage paused, partly to trick the surviving defenders into thinking that the ground attack was beginning and thus draw them out of their cover, and partly to allow the German artillery observers to assess the damage they had inflicted. When the bombardment restarted the smaller calibre weapons commenced pounding the surviving stretches of the French front line, while the 210mm batteries lengthened their range. In all the barrage lasted for nine hours, and

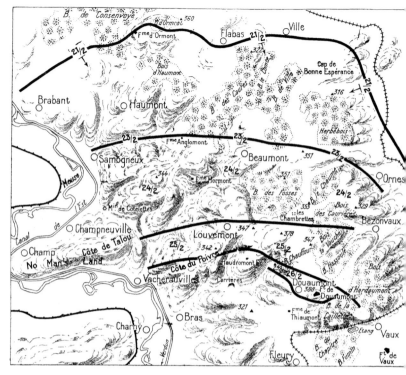

14 The initial German attack, 21–26 February 1916.

the tempo increased yet further for the final hour; in some places around 80,000 shells fell in every 5,000 square yards of the French forward zone.[49] The barrage finally lifted at 16.00, and German assault infantry began moving forward along an eight-mile front east of the River Meuse toward the French 30th Corps front running through, from west to east, the Bois d'Haumont, Bois de Caures and the Bois d'Herebois. Equipped with white armbands for quick recognition in the gloom and with the spikes removed from their Pickelhaube helmets to prevent them catching in the heavy brush, they picked their way forward in small groups through a smoking moonscape littered with fallen trees. Some were armed with the new and terrifying *Flammenwerfer* (flame-throwers), while others carried oxyacetylene cutters to deal with tangles of French barbed wire. These were fighting patrols rather than a full-scale advance, for Falkenhayn had decreed the initial move should be restricted to locating gaps and surviving defenders in the shattered French lines in preparation for a full-scale advance on the following day. The delay appears to have been part of his bleeding strategy, and was likely intended to allow the French to bring up reinforcements for destruction.

However, the westernmost German formation, General von Zwehl's 7th Reserve Corps, had other ideas. Von Zwehl intended to seize a significant foothold from the outset, and his men thus infiltrated the Bois d'Haumont before Lieutenant-Colonel Bonviolle's 165th RI could react, flowing around and eliminating pockets of French resistance like an incoming feldgrau tide and securing the wood in its entirety in five hours. The new Flammenwerfer provoked panic wherever they were employed, with one team taking the surrender of a French officer and thirty-six men. The assault troops made similar progress into the Bois d'Herebois held by the 51st DI at the eastern end of the assault frontage, where the flame-throwers again caused panic and at least one rout. Matters unfolded a little differently in the centre, where Lieutenant-Colonel Driant held the Bois de Caures with the 400 or so light infantrymen from the 56th and 59th BCP who survived the barrage. His forward positions were held by a company under a twenty-three-year-old Lieutenant Robin, which fought hand-to-hand until driven back by superior numbers. As French doctrine demanded, Robin then organised an after dark counter-attack with the eighty survivors, which ejected the Germans and took several prisoners. Driant himself left his partially demolished command post with a rifle as soon as the alarm was raised and set about rallying his stunned soldiers with the words 'We're here, it's our position, and we're not moving from it.'[50]

The confused fighting slackened with the onset of darkness, which brought more snow. The French resistance was an unwelcome shock to the German infantry, who had been told nothing would survive the bombardment. This was especially the case at the Bois des Caures, where Driant's little band rebuffed all German attempts to infiltrate their positions. The 165th RI spent the night preparing to retake the Bois d'Haumont, but 72nd DI HQ postponed the attempt to 05.00 and then 08.30 while they strove to gather reinforcements. Many of these were annihilated by the German bombardment, which recommenced in all its fury just after dawn, and von Zwehl's 7th Corps took the initiative once again by launching a full-scale advance south from the Bois d'Haumont behind the barrage rather than waiting for it to lift. Lieutenant-Colonel Bonviolle cancelled the attack but the word did not reach a depleted company commanded by a Lieutenant Derome, who led a courageous but futile charge into the wall of German shellfire and the full German division advancing behind it. There were only fifty survivors, a badly wounded Derome among them. Von Zwehl's troops rolled on and by nightfall had secured the village of Haumont, almost two miles from their start line, after an intensive barrage and house-to-house fighting that wiped out the 165th RI with a loss of 1,800 men. Bonviolle led five officers and less than sixty men to safety.[51]

Lieutenant-Colonel Driant's little band of light infantrymen spent the night trying to shore up their shattered defences, although their efforts were rent asunder by the German guns when they recommenced the bombardment at 07.00. When it lifted at midday they were facing the full might of the German 17th Corps, which had been reprimanded by von Knobelsdorf for its tardy performance the previous day. Driant's men contested every inch of ground, resorting to rifle butts and even stones when their ammunition gave out. They inflicted over 400 casualties on the German first wave, the heaviest loss on the whole front, but the sheer weight of numbers meant the unequal fight could have only one end. By the late afternoon Driant and around eighty men were besieged in his command post, pleas for support and reinforcement had gone unanswered, and they had no answer at all when the Germans manhandled two 77mm field guns up to shell them from close range. Driant burned his papers while someone else punctured the regimental rum barrel, and then led one of three groups toward safety through the gathering gloom. He was killed on the way after giving aid to one of his wounded men, and the Battle of Verdun gained its first icon.

The dogged defence of the Bois des Caures disjointed the German 17th Corps's timetable for a second time, and the sole effective French artillery barrage of the day disrupted the German assault on the Bois d'Herebois to the east. Nonetheless, by the end of the day the Germans had overrun the whole French front line as far south as Beaumont, apart from the anchor point on the Meuse at Brabant, which was almost encircled by the German advance from Haumont to Samogneux. The latter fell the next day when the Germans broke through the French second line, and a misunderstanding led to a withdrawal from the section of front line facing east over the Woëvre Plain. By midnight on 24 February the German advance had overrun the French first and second lines and Falkenhayn's attrition strategy was working well. General Adrien Chrétien's 30th Corps, which had borne the brunt of the German assault, was virtually destroyed. The 72nd DI had lost 9,828 men killed, wounded and missing and the 51st DI a total of 6,396.[52] Perhaps more importantly, the fighting was drawing in French reinforcements and Falkenhayn's insistence on a step-by-step advance was allowing them time to arrive. The largely North African 37th DI was thrown in piecemeal from 24 February, and within thirty-six hours lost 4,700 men, and frantic efforts were underway to get General Maurice Balfourier's

20th Corps into the line. Balfourier was preceded by his two leading brigades, which arrived at Verdun in the early hours of the same day after a gruelling forced march, but without machine guns and with only limited ammunition. Despite this and the protests of the brigade commanders, Chrétien pushed both formations straight into the line without food or rest.

The seemingly inexorable German advance was also starting to adversely affect French morale. A combination of the hellish bombardment, freezing conditions and being parcelled out to unfamiliar commanders caused many of the 37th DI's North African soldiers to abandon their posts. Two 240mm guns, one at Vaux and the other at Cumières west of the Meuse, were destroyed by nervous crews. Although it was due to the German bombardment, the paucity of French counter-fire raised suspicions among the infantry that their artillery was being withdrawn and they were being abandoned to their fate. Most damaging of all was the treatment of the wounded. French medical provision was barely adequate at best,[53] and virtually collapsed under the pressure. There were few shelters at the clearing station at Bras to protect the casualties from the constant shellfire, insufficient ambulances to evacuate more than a handful at a time, and the four-mile journey back to Verdun could take twelve hours, if it was made safely at all. Conditions were little better at the base hospitals there, for the German 380mm naval guns had cut the railway line to Châlons and there were again only a handful of ambulances to carry casualties further afield.

By 25 February the German tide was thus lapping at the outer ring of Verdun's fixed defences. Fort Douaumont ought to have presented a formidable if not impregnable obstacle to further German advance. However, as we have seen, the fort had been stripped of almost all its armament, and by the time Gericht began its garrison had been reduced to a mere fifty-six elderly gunners under a warrant officer and a lone sapper sergeant. As a result what had been touted as the most modern and sophisticated fortification in the world fell without a fight to Infanterie Regiment 24 in the late afternoon of 25 February. Credit at the time went to Captain Haupt and First Lieutenant von Brandis, who were awarded Germany's highest gallantry award, the *Pour le Mérite*, by the Kaiser in person. However, the first officer involved appears to have been a somewhat less photogenic Second Lieutenant called Radtke, and the real conqueror of Fort Douaumont was a stolid pioneer NCO named Kunze who did the deed in a manner more suited to a comic opera than a military operation. Blown into the moat by the blast from a near miss and armed only with a pistol, Kunze was deserted by his men

15 Refugees from the Verdun area moving south toward safety. The remaining civilians in Verdun were evacuated at the start of the German attack on 21 February.

after climbing into one of the unmanned machine gun galleries. Undeterred, he penetrated into the fort alone, arresting the crew of the fort's single 155mm gun who promptly escaped, and locking up a group undergoing a lecture who also escaped while Kunze treated himself to a meal in a deserted mess. By that time the three officers had arrived independently and his contribution and that of Radtke was not recognised until after the war. The latter received a signed photograph of the exiled Crown Prince for his trouble while Kunze, by then a policeman, was rewarded with accelerated promotion to inspector.

The French tried to minimise the loss by issuing misleading reports, concentrating on the losses inflicted on the Germans, and then claiming that the fort had been demolished and was no more than a useless ruin in any case. In Germany, however, the news was celebrated with newspaper headlines, bell ringing and a special holiday for schoolchildren, and they also scattered propaganda leaflets proclaiming their coup over French lines. The latter struck a serious blow against already shaky French morale. Fearing being cut off by the fall of Douaumont, the 37th DI withdrew from key positions

16 Damage inflicted by the German bombardment of Verdun.

on two hills, the Côte de Talou and the Côte du Poivre, north-west of the fort. Surviving troops from the 51st DI refused to leave the Verdun barracks where they had been lodged to re-organise. The flow of deserters seeking shelter in Verdun increased markedly and an officer was arrested while running through the streets of the town crying '*Sauve qui peut!*' The Meuse bridges were prepared for demolition, Verdun's remaining civilian population was evacuated, and looting broke out in their wake.

Operation Gericht thus pushed the French to crisis point within five days and the situation was only prevented from spiralling further out of control by a second intervention from Joffre's chief-of-staff, de Castelnau. The latter persuaded a curiously uninterested Joffre of the gravity of the situation on 24 February and arrived in Verdun with full executive authority in the early hours of the following day. By the afternoon he had conducted a rapid but thorough tour of the front, assessed the situation salvable and issued the necessary instructions to bring the situation under control. With hindsight this was a momentous decision, for in so doing so he unwittingly committed the French Army to the role of guinea pig in Falkenhayn's experiment in deliberate attrition. At this point it was feasible for the French to cut their losses by abandoning their foothold east of the Meuse and Verdun itself in favour of a fighting withdrawal to more defensible terrain in the Argonne. This would have been the most logical course from a military perspective, but logic was about to become subsumed in the less straightforward matter of national morale, honour and prestige.

Be that as it may, the most crucial of de Castelnau's instructions was to the French 2nd Army, recently withdrawn from the line and commanded by Major-General Philippe Pétain. Once Captain Serrigny, his aide-de-camp, had tracked him down entertaining a female companion in a Paris hotel room, Pétain was ordered to proceed to Verdun forthwith. Although dictated largely by an accident of availability, Pétain was the perfect choice for the job. As his pre-war criticism of the doctrine of offensive *à l'outrance* showed, he fully understood the relationship between attrition and firepower. Perhaps more importantly, given the tenuous state of French morale at Verdun, he was also popular with the rank-and-file poilu,[54] for despite his aloof and formal manner Pétain had a reputation for husbanding lives and taking care over the welfare of his soldiers. This is clear from the reaction of General Balfourier, commander of the newly arrived 20th Corps, to a telephone call from Pétain informing

17 Major-General Philippe Pétain, commander of the French 2nd Army, at his HQ at Souilly, fourteen miles south-west of Verdun. The officer in the dark uniform is Marshal Joseph Joffre, Commander in Chief of the French Army.

of the change of command: 'Is that you, my general? That's good! Now everything is going to be alright.'[55]

Pétain arrived in Verdun in the afternoon of 25 February. After a brief meeting with the overwhelmed General Herr, who was verging on a breakdown, he set off to establish his own HQ at Souilly, fourteen miles south-west of Verdun on the road to Bar-le-Duc. At around 23.00 he ran into de Castelnau who had already decreed Pétain was to take command of all forces at Verdun with effect from midnight, and ordered him to hold the east bank of the Meuse at all costs. Pétain then continued to the mairie (town hall) at Souilly and traced the line to be held for his chief-of-staff Colonel Maurice de Barescut. It was to be divided into four sectors. General George Bazelaire was placed in command of the line west of the Meuse, between Avocourt and the river. On the east bank, General Marie Louis Guillaumat was responsible for the area running east from the Meuse to Douaumont village; General Balfourier for the sector between Douaumont and the point where the line curved south near Damloup; and General Duchesne for the sector facing the Woëvre Plain. That done, Pétain telephoned Balfourier and Bazelaire

18 French troops resting in the ruins of Douaumont village, the focus of heavy fighting immediately after the fall of Fort Douaumont on 25 February 1916. The village changed hands several times before finally falling to the Germans on 4 March 1916, by which time it had been reduced to rubble.

before retiring for a few hours' sleep, and promptly came down with a severe case of double pneumonia. He spent the next few days controlling the battle from his sickbed through de Barescut and Serrigny, while his staff strove to keep their chief's illness secret.

Pétain thus arrived at a crisis point in the battle for Verdun, as the Germans strove to maintain their momentum and capitalise on their capture of Fort Douaumont. The nearby village of the same name was reduced to rubble before finally falling on 4 March, after changing hands several times, being pounded with 420mm guns and with significant loss to both sides. The 95th RI was virtually destroyed there on 25 February followed by Pétain's old command the 33rd RI, which lost a third of its strength within three days. One German *Jäger* battalion lost 413 men on 27 February alone, a Prussian Leib Grenadier battalion was reduced to 196 men, and by 2 March another regiment had lost 38 officers and 1,151 men.[56] Measures orchestrated by Pétain from his sickbed caused the Germans yet more friction. The line west of Douaumont was secured by elements of Balfourier's 20th Corps re-occupying the Côte du Poivre before the Germans could take advantage of the precipitate withdrawal of the 37th DI. They were supported by a number of field guns, pushed right up to the front near the *Ouvrage de Froideterre* and firing virtually over open sights.

Pétain also reversed the policy toward the forts and smaller works, despatching guns and infantry with instructions to defend them to the death. He ordered the inner line of forts protecting Verdun, Forts Tavannes, Souville and Belleville, to be linked with trenches as a last-ditch backstop position; this was dubbed the 'Panic Line' by the troops detailed to do the digging. In line with his pre-war dictum that firepower killed, Pétain paid special attention to building the French artillery into a force capable of meeting its German opponent on equal terms. He massed large numbers of guns west of the Meuse from where they could pour fire into the German troops as they crossed the ravines running down to the river. Many were emplaced within or near the forts on the Bois de Bourrus ridge, where they were protected from German counter-fire. French shelling stopped one German advance over the Côte de Talou in its tracks and killed the German 3rd Corps's artillery commander, General Lotterer, as he supervised his own guns.

Important as all this was, Pétain's most crucial contribution was in line with the adage that amateurs study tactics while professionals study logistics, and was thus concerned with maintaining the flow of men and materiel into Verdun. This was a vital concern given that the French force was well on the way to numbering half a million

19 French troops and Berliet trucks on the road between Verdun and Bar-le-Duc. Dubbed the *Voie Sacrée* (Sacred Way), this was the only road into Verdun during the battle. Note that the road is occupied solely by motor transport; troops and horsed transport were obliged to keep to the fields on either side.

men with 170,000 draught animals when Pétain assumed command; the latter alone required around 2,000 tons of forage per day. As we have seen, the severing of Verdun's mainline rail links had left the town reliant on the narrow-gauge military railway nicknamed the Meusien and the unmetalled minor road running to Bar-le-Duc, thirty miles to the south-west. By happy accident the road had been widened to seven yards, sufficient to allow two-way motor traffic, in 1915. The engineer officers in charge of the route, Major Richard and Captain Doumenc, had increased the available transport fleet to 3,500 motor trucks, largely by commandeering civilian vehicles across France. This was no mean feat considering that the French Army could only muster a mere 170 motor trucks in 1914. The vehicles were deployed in a system named noria, the French term for an industrial water-wheel. At any given time half the vehicles would be en route to Verdun loaded with supplies, while the other half headed away loaded with relieved units or the wounded.[57]

Pétain lost no time in interviewing Major Richard, ascertaining what he required and ensuring it was forthcoming. The equivalent of a division was thus set to work building a broad-gauge railway to Revigny-sur-Ornain, just north-west of Bar-le-Duc. The road, latter immortalised as the *Voie Sacrée* (Sacred Way), was divided into six self-contained sections, each with its own repair workshops, mechanics, engineers and labour force. The carriageway was reserved exclusively for motor vehicles, with breakdowns being tipped unceremoniously off the road for repair teams to recover later. Horse-drawn transport was banned, presumably to protect the unmade road from being ploughed by hooves, and the columns of heavily laden poilus were restricted to marching through the fields alongside the road. The refined system worked, even when a sudden thaw on 28 February turned the road to liquid mud up to eighteen inches deep. Over the following week 190,000 men and 25,000 tons of supplies flowed north into Verdun, a rate that settled down to a steady weekly flow

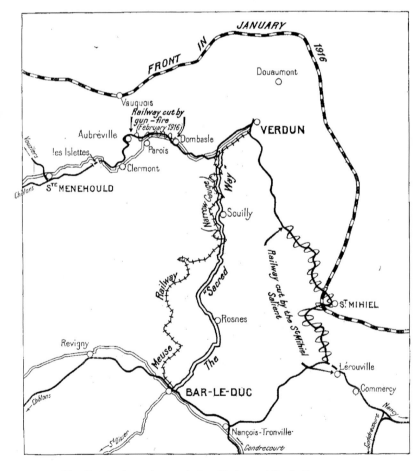

20 The *Voie Sacrée* supply route linking Verdun and Bar-le Duc.

of 90,000 men and 50,000 tons of materiel. Around 10,000 full-time road menders, many from Indo-China and Senegal, were employed in maintaining the road surface using an estimated 750,000 tons of stone over the ten-month span of the battle, much of it shovelled directly under the wheels of the trucks. At its peak of activity in June 1916, 12,000 trucks were moving back and forth along the road around the clock, at rate of one every ten to fourteen seconds.[58]

Gericht began to lose momentum after just over a week due to the effects of non-stop, high intensity operations and increasingly effective French countermeasures. German records noted 27 February as the first day on which their troops took no new ground, and an attempted river crossing near Samogneux to counter the murderous French flanking fire by von Zwehl's VII Reserve Corps failed the same day. By 29 February German losses had equalled the French loss of 25,000 men since the battle began. The German 18th Corps, which had spearheaded the attack into the Bois de Caures on 21 February, had lost 295 officers and 10,309 men by 12 March and had to be withdrawn from the line. This was exacerbated by Falkenhayn's policy of withholding reinforcements, which by 25 February had reduced the 5th Army's reserve to a single regiment to cover its entire frontage. At least equally seriously, the German artillery began to experience difficulty in maintaining its rate of fire. French counter-fire exacted a horrendous price from the German arm's horses, with 7,000 animals being killed in a single day. This and a combination of the broken terrain and mud interfered with ammunition resupply to the extent that some artillery batteries units had to be withdrawn for the want of shells, and infantrymen had to be pressed into service as ammunition bearers for those that remained. The strain of constant firing also began to simply wear out the guns themselves, noticeable by a severe drop in accuracy or worse. A shell detonated in the barrel of one of the 420mm pieces brought forward with huge effort to shell Fort Souville, destroying the gun and killing some of its crew.

5

The Battle Expands West of the Meuse: 6 March–29 May 1916

The end of February was also the point where Gericht expanded beyond the narrow boundaries envisaged by Falkenhayn. On 28 February Crown Prince Wilhelm and von Knobelsdorf persuaded Falkenhayn that the root of the problem was flanking fire from Fort Vaux in the east and the French guns across the Meuse. They thus obtained permission to extend the attack to the west bank of the river with the newly arrived 6th Reserve Corps, with a parallel attack on the east bank toward Fort Vaux scheduled to begin twenty-four hours later. The objective on the west bank was a ridge linking a pair of peaks two miles behind the French lines called locally, with sinister prescience, *Le Mort Homme* (The Dead Man); seizing this feature would expose the French artillery massed on the Bois de Bourrus ridge. The attack was to be two pronged, the main effort being a general advance from the existing front line to the north. This was to be supplemented by a river crossing from the east bank of the Meuse by von Zwehl's 7th Reserve Corps between Brabant and Champneuville.

The French detected German preparations and moved four divisions into the line and allocated a fifth to General Bazelaire's reserve while stockpiling artillery ammunition in anticipation. The attack opened on 6 March 1916 with a barrage as intense as the one that had opened Gericht the previous month. However, this time it was blunted by a heavy French counter-barrage, even though many shells failed to detonate in the soggy ground, and by the end of the day the German advance had barely reached the village of Béthincourt, a third of the way to the Mort Homme. The 7th Reserve Corps's river crossing, which was intended to be a supplementary opera-

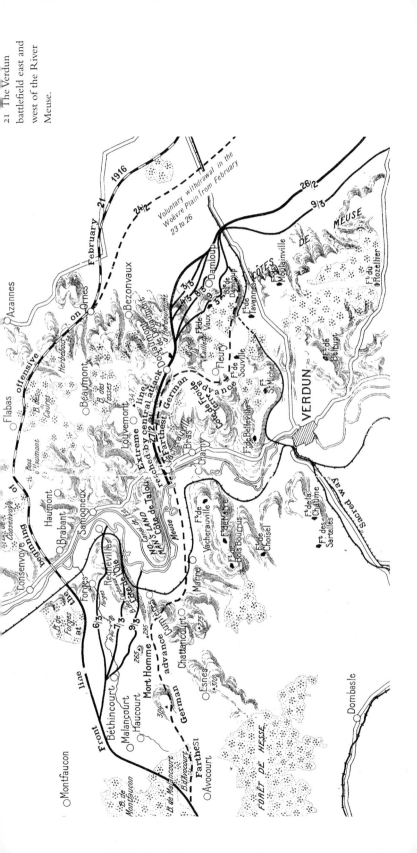

21 The Verdun battlefield east and west of the River Meuse.

22 Shells bursting on the Mort Homme.

tion, went far better. Initially assisted by fire from an armoured train that had been sneaked almost up to the front line, von Zwehl's men quickly occupied Forges and Regneville and seized Point 265 on the Côte de l'Oie (Goose Ridge), which ran west through the Bois de Corbeaux to the end of the Mort Homme. By nightfall on 7 March they had overrun the rest of the wood and had inflicted over 3,000 casualties on the defenders from the 67th DI.

German occupation of the Bois de Corbeaux posed a serious threat to the Mort Homme and Lieutenant-Colonel Macker's 92nd RI was ordered to retake it at dawn on 8 March. Armed with a cane and smoking a cigar Macker led his men across the 400 hundred metres to the wood in person, ordering a bayonet charge at a hundred metres in a textbook demonstration of offensive *à l'outrance* that routed the Germans and secured the wood by 07.20. Macker successfully performed the same trick again two days later, but his luck ran out and he was killed after going forward to congratulate one of his battalion commanders. A rapid German riposte then recaptured the Bois de Corbeaux after intense fighting that reduced one German battalion to 300 men, but stiff French resistance prevented further advance. An attempt to renew the attack toward Béthincourt on 9 March made minimal progress for maximum cost, as did the parallel attack on Fort Vaux over on the east bank of the Meuse. Also launched on 9 March, two days behind schedule due to a shortage of artillery ammunition, that assault bogged down in the rubble of Vaux village, which changed hands no less than thirteen times. The cost to the Germans was exacerbated by a rash attempt to occupy Fort Vaux following a rumour that it was undefended like Fort Douaumont. The German divisional commander involved, having despatched a suitably glowing report of his part in the imminent triumph to 5th

Army HQ, tried to march his men onto the fully manned fort's glacis in column. The result was both predictable and fatal for many of the soldiers involved.

French propagandists seized on the German reverse at Fort Vaux to ease their embarrassment over Douaumont, while the GQG and Joffre began talking of counter-offensives on the assumption that the German attack had run out of steam. This was wishful thinking, for the latter renewed their efforts against the Mort Homme on 14 March with six full divisions. Within a week this had in turn spawned yet another westward expansion of the battlefront, this time to nullify French artillery emplaced on a flanking height dubbed Côte 304. The new assault was entrusted to Infanterie Division 11 and was aimed at a heavily fortified section of the line in the Bois d'Avocourt three miles west of Côte 304. German preparations were assisted by French deserters from the unit holding the Bois d'Avocourt, the 29th DI, and included excavating mines under the French positions. In the event, the mines failed to detonate when the attack went in on 20 March but the demoralised 29th DI crumbled under the assault. Infanterie Division 11 secured the entire wood in four hours, capturing an entire French brigade of 2,825 men in the process.[59] Heavy rain then turned the battlefield into a quagmire, and the pendulum of attrition swung back against the Germans when their next attack on 22 March was stopped cold by well-sited French machine guns with the loss of 2,400 men. A French attempt to repair the damage to their line on 29 March only regained a corner of the wood.

By the end of March 1916 the fighting on the west bank of the Meuse had cost the lives of 81,607 German and 89,000 French soldiers. The lack of forts or other permanent fortifications on or around Côte 304 and the Mort Homme compelled the French to rely solely on trenches, which were simply erased by the sheer intensity of the German barrage. Shellfire ploughed the battlefield into a moonscape of churned mud and shattered trees, burying men and equipment, cutting telephone wires and killing messengers, forcing commanders to rely on pigeons for communication. The front line was reduced to small groups of men clinging to hastily linked clusters of shell craters. The strain was also beginning to tell on both sides. One otherwise healthy French lieutenant-colonel died suddenly of a heart attack, and German medical officers began to express concern over the mental and physical condition of their troops. There were also disquieting rumours of German units giving up too easily or even refusing to advance when ordered.[60] A senior NCO from Infanterie Regiment 243 complained in his diary that he and his

23 The remains of Malancourt after the fighting on 31 March 1916.

24 Fully manned French trench on the Mort Homme after its recapture in August 1917. Note the dug-out entrance on the left.

25 Trench on the Mort Homme. The sparse manning and relatively shallow depth suggests a communication trench on the lower slopes of the hill.

comrades had been misled by their superiors and had given up hope of ever reaching Verdun, for example.[61] Nonetheless, the German attack on the west bank ground remorselessly on. Malancourt fell on 31 March, Haucourt on 5 April and Béthincourt three days later, bringing the German advance to the foot of Côte 304.

While all this was going on, the Germans were preparing a further large-scale effort. Scheduled to begin on 9 April, it was to be a properly co-ordinated thrust down both banks of the Meuse simultaneously. The German command structure had been rationalised, with General Bruno von Mudra being placed in command of forces east of the Meuse while General Max von Gallwitz, an artillery specialist newly arrived from the Balkan front, took over the sector west of the river. The preparatory German bombardment on the Mort Homme and Côte 304 consumed seventeen trainloads of ammunition and the attack added several thousand more casualties to the total, with one German division alone losing 2,200 men.[62] It also finally reached the summit of the Mort Homme as marked on German maps; unfortunately the real crest lay another thirty metres up the slope. Despite the German attack being the heaviest since the battle began on 21 February, the French held their line, as did their comrades on the east bank, where a heavy German attack on the Côte du Poivre near Douaumont was also repulsed. This prompted Pétain to issue a stirring Order of the Day that ended with his famous paraphrase from Joan of Arc: '*Courage! On les aura!*' (Courage! We will beat them!).

The weather then intervened, and heavy rain forced a pause in the fighting for the better part of two weeks as the troops struggled with the resultant mud and flooded trenches and shell craters. This gave von Gallwitz time to prepare for his next move, which included digging two mile-long tunnels, dubbed 'Gallwitz' and 'Kronprinz', to protect German troops moving up to the line on the Mort Homme in safety. The initial effort was made against Côte 304, however, because French guns ensconced behind the feature had again been instrumental in blunting the attack on 9 April. On 3 May over 500 guns began a thirty-six-hour bombardment of a mile-long stretch of the French line, sending a column of dust and smoke over 2,000 feet into the air. Even then the German assault troops ran into determined resistance, and the summit was not secured until 7 May after bitter close-quarter fighting. Overall the fight for Côte 304 cost an estimated 10,000 French lives; by the end of April the Gericht toll had risen to 120,000 German and 133,000 French casualties.[63] The stage was thus set for the capture of the Mort Homme. French counter-attacks had driven back the German gains from their attack on 9 April, but the Germans finally secured the ridge in its entirety on 29 May 1916. It had taken eighty-four days, tens of thousands of lives – overall French losses had topped the 185,000 mark by the end of May – and hundreds of thousands of artillery shells to secure a strip of land seven miles long and three miles deep.

26 French troops in a trench on Côte 304.

27 French aid post located in a dug-out on Côte 304.

6

Attrition and Reappraisals: 28 February–1 June 1916

The Germans were thus finally free to return their attention to the east bank of the Meuse, where the line had barely moved as both sides strove to gain or maintain tactical advantage under an almost continuous rain of shells. Most of this was concentrated in an area south of Fort Douaumont dubbed the 'Deadly Quadrilateral'. On the German side Falkenhayn appeared to be losing interest in his experiment in attrition, but on 4 April he nonetheless authorised Crown Prince Wilhelm to renew the attack east of the Meuse. A combination of the ongoing French resistance on the heights west of the Meuse, bad weather and the failure of a series of limited attacks in the Quadrilateral delayed this, and paralleled the Crown Prince's growing sense of disillusionment. A pessimistic review by von Mudra in mid-April led the Crown Prince and the majority of

28 Aerial photograph of Fort Douaumont taken in May 1916.

the 5th Army staff to conclude by 21 April that Gericht had failed and ought to be terminated, and a huge accidental explosion in Fort Douaumont on 8 May reinforced the gloom yet further. Allegedly caused by soldiers brewing coffee on a table improvised from boxes of explosive using the explosive filling of a hand-grenade for fuel, a chain reaction detonated stockpiled German ammunition and Flammenwerfer canisters and then spread to the fort's ammunition magazine. The blasts killed 679 men, including the entire staff of Grenadier Regiment 12. Some who survived the blast and escaped from the fort interior were machine-gunned by their own side, their soot-blackened faces being mistaken for feared French African troops in the confusion.

However, the real power at 5th Army was von Knobelsdorf, who had been appointed by the Kaiser to keep an eye on the inexperienced Crown Prince. Knobelsdorf remained convinced that Gericht was not only viable but the correct course, and so von Mudra was replaced as commander east of the Meuse by General Ewald von Lochow. Knobelsdorf also engineered the removal of the Crown Prince's supportive personal staff officer, Lieutenant-Colonel von Heymann, and he deliberately misrepresented Wilhelm's position to Falkenhayn after agreeing to argue the case for a termination of Gericht in person on his behalf. Falkenhayn also sidelined the Crown Prince's reservations when he visited 5th Army HQ in mid-May. In desperation Wilhelm turned to his father, but this was unsuccessful due to their difficult personal relationship which left the Crown Prince unable to broach the matter in person, and the Kaiser had a long-standing practice of merely redirecting written communications from his son to the appropriate military department. Preparations for what was to be an even more intense phase of the battle thus continued despite his misgivings and disillusionment.

Developments on the French side were also conspiring to exacerbate the intensity of the fighting. The root of the problem there was a growing disenchantment between Joffre and Pétain. By May 1916 fifty-two French divisions were deployed around Verdun, and forty of them had been cycled through the heaviest fighting at least once. This was a deliberate policy, for Pétain had noted that leaving units in the line for long periods had a deleterious effect on their battle-worthiness and morale. His noria replacement system thus relieved them after a few days, before casualties and morale became an issue and rotated them back for rest and recuperation. None of this particularly impressed Joffre however, who became frustrated with what he perceived to be a lack of aggression on Pétain's part, and a fear that the ongoing battle at Verdun would interfere with

29 General Robert Nivelle,
Commander of the French
3rd Corps which arrived at
Verdun at the end of March
1916. He was later promoted
to command the French
2nd Army when Pétain
moved on to take command
of Army Group Centre in
April 1916.

his plans for a summer offensive on the Somme. For his part, Pétain
thought that French efforts should be concentrated at Verdun rather
than elsewhere, and was determined to avoid having the lives husbanded by the noria system squandered in piecemeal counter-attacks
that owed more to doctrinal dogma than tactical necessity or even
common sense.

The latter was a particular concern on the east bank after the
arrival of General Robert Nivelle's 3rd Corps at the end of March
1916. Nivelle was an enthusiastic proponent of offensive *à l'outrance*,
as was his senior divisional commander General Charles Mangin,
whose diligence in this regard had earned him the grim nickname of
le boucher (the butcher) from the men under his command. Nivelle's
formation started as it intended to continue; Mangin threw in an
impromptu attack against the Bois de la Caillette south of Fort
Douaumont on the day his 5th DI began its first stint in the line, and
before it had fully arrived. Such small-scale attacks became an almost
daily occurrence and gained the area south of Fort Douaumont
its label of the Deadly Quadrilateral, while Pétain tried to rein in
Nivelle and his subordinate with limited success.

Ordinarily Joffre would have simply sacked Pétain and replaced
him with someone more amenable. Indeed, such action had become
so commonplace in the French army that it received its own verb,

limoger, after the practice of sending relieved officers to the town of Limoges in western France for reassignment. However, more circumspection was required in this instance, as Pétain's status as the saviour of Verdun made direct action politically imprudent. Joffre therefore took the more creative approach of promoting Pétain to command Army Group Centre on 19 April and, having been favourably impressed by Nivelle on a visit to his HQ ten days earlier, gave him Pétain's job at the head of the 2nd Army. To add insult to injury Joffre also discontinued the noria system shortly afterward. Pétain was thus placed in the invidious position of having to watch as his careful work was undone and the units he had nurtured and husbanded were squandered. The situation on the French side was thus a mirror image of that on the other side of the front line, with the bellicose winning out over more moderate while the battle and attendant death toll ran on remorselessly. Interestingly, the idea that the battle had somehow taken on a life of its own and was running beyond human agency or control began to appear among contemporary comment on both sides at around this time.[64]

Neither were Nivelle and Mangin slow in taking up the opportunity to expand their aggressive activities, and the focus of their attention was the German-held Fort Douaumont. The Germans had opened new entrances into the northern side of the fort, which they used as a shelter and conduit for troops moving between the front line and rear at an average of a thousand per night. The justification for their interest was thus the need to remove the fort as an enemy conduit and because it provided an observation point over French

30 General Charles Mangin, commander of the 5th *Division d'Infanterie* and subsequently the 3rd Corps comprising all French units on the east bank of the River Meuse. Technically competent but ruthless in the extreme, Mangin was nicknamed *le boucher* (the butcher) by his men.

positions, but the prospect of glory for reconquering it also appears to have been a significant motivation. Be that as it may, Mangin made his first attempt to regain the fort on 22 April and his men actually reached its superstructure before being driven back. Undaunted, Mangin began agitating for permission to launch a stronger and more carefully planned effort after witnessing the aftermath of the accidental explosion inside Douaumont on 8 May. Nivelle agreed immediately and Pétain reluctantly followed suit under pressure from Joffre. Scheduled for 22 May, the attack was to be conducted by the 74th and 129th RIs on a mere 1,000-metre frontage, supported by 290 guns including a number of brand new 370mm mortars.[65] Mangin may have been ruthless but he was also extremely technically competent, and he visited Fort Moulainville to ascertain the best way of attacking Douaumont. He was less than impressed when the Commandant of the fort pointed out that 370mm mortars were unlikely to make much impression as Moulainville had recently withstood prolonged shelling from German 420mm pieces.

The French preparatory bombardment went on for five days, dropping 1,000 tons of shells per day on Douaumont. The barrage obliterated a German signal station established on the fort glacis, destroyed the surviving observation domes and machine gun turrets and opened a breach in the roof of the west-facing Casemate de Bourges. Shell-shocked men wandered the fume- and dust-filled corridors, which were plunged into darkness when a near miss brought the roof down on the solitary generator, and the fort rapidly filled with injured men as the barrage took a dreadful toll of the German troops posted in the trenches outside. Based on this Mangin could be forgiven for telling one of his battalion commanders that the assault would be a walkover. However, appearances were deceptive, and not merely because the five-day barrage effectively removed any element of surprise. Security at Nivelle's HQ was extremely lax, and the Germans were fully conversant with every detail of the French plan within two days of the orders being issued on 13 May. They promptly ceased all other operations on the east bank of the Meuse in anticipation.

This became apparent to the French assault troops when the Germans dropped two perfectly aimed ranging shells into their jumping-off trenches half an hour before the assault was scheduled to begin. They thus ran straight into a murderous counter-barrage as soon as they left their trenches. An entire battalion from the 74th RI was annihilated, another was stopped cold, and every company in the 129th RI was reduced to around forty-five men or less in a matter of minutes. Mangin himself was almost killed by a shell burst that wounded four of his staff officers while watching the action from atop Fort Souville. Incredibly, the 74th RI's third battalion reached its objective on the right flank of the fort. Even more incredibly the severely depleted members of the 129th RI managed to reach the fort in eleven minutes. Within half an hour they had seized most of the fort superstructure, and a machine gun set up on the roof of the Casemate de Bourges was repulsing the first of many German forays from within the fort. In addition, small parties of French troops penetrated into the fort interior via the breached roof and quickly reached the broad central corridor that linked the various parts of the fort.

All the initial signs suggested that Fort Douaumont was back in French hands, and Mangin wasted no time in reporting to Nivelle's HQ with a list of officers recommended for promotion and decoration for their part in the triumph. This proved to be somewhat optimistic, however. The French interlopers inside the fort were soon driven back to the outlying passages, and counter-attacks against the French troops clinging to the fort glacis and right flank went on throughout 23 May. Equally critically, the German artillery erected a near impermeable barrage between them and reinforcements; a major effort from the 124th RI managed to reach the German front line but were driven back with the loss of 500 men. In the afternoon the little pocket from the 74th RI, which by this time had lost almost three-quarters of its strength, was encircled and forced to surrender. This left the men from the 129th RI isolated atop the fort but still holding out by nightfall, thanks largely to the machine gun on the roof of the Casemate de Bourges. The Germans used the cover of darkness to emplace a large-calibre Minenwerfer only eighty yards away, and at dawn on 24 May rapidly lobbed eight rounds onto the French machine gun in quick succession before overrunning the surviving French interlopers.

In all, the fighting on and around Fort Douaumont netted the Germans a thousand prisoners.[66] A few French survivors crept back to friendly lines in ones and twos over the next day or so, but Mangin's 5th DI had been virtually destroyed in what proved to be its bloodiest action of the war, which cost 900 dead, 2,900 wounded and a further 1,600 missing.[67] This in turn left a dangerous vacuum in the French front that extended beyond that formation's frontage. Overall, the French suffered higher casualties at Verdun in the last two weeks of May than any similar period since the battle began, to the extent that nine of the seventeen divisions in the line had to be relieved.[68] Ironically, given his reservations about the attack, Pétain took full responsibility for the reverse, and Mangin was relieved of his command for rounding on his immediate superior, General Leonce Lebrun, when the latter insisted Mangin continue the attack.[69]

There were two more serious consequences to set alongside the weakening of the French front and the cost tallied in the list of dead, wounded, missing and prisoners. First, the rebuff at Douaumont was accompanied by disquieting reports of *défaillance* (weakness or breakdown) among the French troops involved, mirroring similar manifestations among their opponents during the earlier fighting for the Mort Homme and Côte 304 across the Meuse. Second, it rekindled Falkenhayn's flagging interest in his experiment in attrition. An officer visiting the latter's HQ while the French attack on Fort Douaumont was underway found the usually taciturn and distant Falkenhayn uncharacteristically animated, declaring that the French were behaving in a stupid but accommodating manner. He therefore put his full support behind the 5th Army's upcoming assault on the French line east of the Meuse being planned by von Knobelsdorf and the wavering Crown Prince. Codenamed 'May Cup' and scheduled to start at the beginning of June 1916, the attack was to be the heaviest German effort since the battle opened the previous February. It was intended to seize the final jumping point for the capture of Verdun by securing Fort Souville and the Fleury ridge on the brink of the Meuse Heights overlooking the town, using the 1st, 10th Reserve and 15th Corps. Five divisions were to carry out the initial assault on a three-mile frontage, with a troop density of one man per yard. This time there was to be no finesse or infiltration tactics, just a head-on assault intended to batter its way through the French defences with firepower and sheer weight of numbers.

The latter was maximised by the Germans temporarily regaining artillery superiority. By the end of May von Knobelsdorf had amassed 2,200 guns to the French 1,177, although the advantage was not quite as clear cut as the bare numbers suggested. This was particularly the case with the German 420mm howitzers, whose performance had been severely degraded by the time of May Cup. Their barrels were simply worn out, having had far more shells put through them than the manufacturers had envisaged as the limit of their useful life. At best this caused shells to 'keyhole' or tumble end-over-end after being fired, with obvious implications for accuracy and penetration. At worst it could cause shells to detonate prematurely in or as they emerged from the barrel, as happened to one gun shelling Fort Souville at the end of February. The Germans had exacerbated the problem by using the guns to shell Fort Moulainville, which was of marginal relevance to what was happening at the front. This diversion also had unexpected consequences after one round failed to explode after hitting the fort; French ballistic experts were able to swiftly back-calculate the trajectory to pinpoint the gun and bring it under fire. Several 420s fell victim to increasingly effective French counter-battery fire, not least because of their huge size and consequent immobility, and on one occasion a swift counter-fire mission destroyed a German ammunition dump containing almost half a million shells in the Bois de Spincourt. By the beginning of June the 5th Army had only four 420mm pieces left of the thirteen with which they had started the battle.

The major obstacle between the Germans and their final jumping-off point against Verdun was Fort Vaux and three concrete-reinforced strongpoints covering the west and north-western approaches to Vaux; flanking fire from the latter had proved decisive in rebuffing previous German attacks on the fort. Located in the Bois de la Caillette and Bois de Fumin, these covering positions were called Retranchement 1 to 3, with R1 being only 400 metres west of the fort covering the approaches to its glacis. Vaux was the smallest fully-fledged fort in the ring around Verdun. A tapered rectangle in plan, sixty metres to a side, it was almost a quarter-scale replica of Douaumont, equipped with a single 75mm turret and girdled with a concrete ditch with machine gun galleries set into the outer faces of the south-western, north-western and north-eastern corners. Capable of sweeping the ditch with fire, these were linked by tunnel to the fort interior. By June the 75mm turret had been destroyed

31 Aerial photograph of Fort Vaux. Note the German trenches running close to the front (top of picture) and west sides of the fort, established at the beginning of March 1916.

when a huge emergency demolition charge placed there in the aftermath of the fall of Douaumont was detonated by a near miss from a 420mm shell. Repeated shelling had also opened up wide cracks in the fort's reinforced concrete structure, and a direct hit had opened up the roof of one of the corridors linking the galleries to the fort; the gap was hastily plugged with sandbags.

The fort was commanded by Major Sylvain-Eugene Raynal, a long-serving officer relegated to fortress duty after sustaining several serious wounds that left him reliant on a walking stick. Raynal arrived on 24 May 1916 and found that despite Pétain's order at the end of February, no tunnel had been dug to protect troops entering and leaving the fort; neither had any measures been taken to improve the fort's water supply, which proved to be Vaux's Achilles heel. This was all the more serious because the fort was crammed with a variety of wounded, stretcher bearers, signallers and stragglers from units stationed in the trenches around the fort. Efforts to clear these men out proved fruitless because those evicted either returned or were rapidly replaced by others understandably seeking shelter from the incessant shelling outside. Thus at the beginning of June, when the Germans resumed the offensive, there were still around 600 men crammed into a fort designed for a garrison of 250, along with a lone spaniel and four carrier pigeons.

7

Resuming the Offensive:
1–23 June 1916

Operation May Cup began on Thursday, 1 June 1916. The advance on Fort Vaux came from the north-west through the Bois de la Caillette, and was intended to remove the protective strongpoints in the Bois de la Caillette and Bois de Fumin in preparation for moving on the fort proper. Handicapped by the loss of the 75mm turret there was little Raynal could do to help, although two machine guns firing at high elevation and extreme range from the glacis inflicted a number of casualties on German troops moving into the Bois de la Caillette. The Germans had expected it to take four days to deal with the strongpoints in the woods, but the speed of the advance far outpaced expectations.

By the late afternoon of 1 June only the R1 strongpoint, held by a company from the 101st RI under Captain Charles Delvert, remained in French hands. All but surrounded, Delvert's company was reduced to seventy-one men by 3 June, and was unable to interfere effectively with German assaults on Fort Vaux. Attempts to reinforce Delvert were stymied by German shelling; of two companies despatched as reinforcements on 3 June, only eighteen and twenty-five men respectively got through. The defenders withstood repeated German attacks, shelling by French artillery and the torment of thirst, allaying the latter by catching rain in their groundsheets on the night of 5 June. Delvert was finally relieved later that night of 5/6 June, although German machine gun fire and shelling en route reduced his force to thirty-seven by the time they finally reached safety; they had inflicted an estimated 300 casualties on their German attackers. Their departure came none too soon, as a German assault on 9 June finally overran R1, taking 500 French prisoners in the process.

The commander of the German 15th Corps, General Berthold von Deimling, moved swiftly to capitalise on the rapid advance on

32a and bThe German effort to reduce Fort Vaux began by dealing with French supporting positions to the north-west, which included the village of Vaux. Contrast the intact state of the village in January 1916 with a picture from April 1917, after the German attacks at the beginning of March and June 1916 had virtually wiped the village from the face of the earth.

1 June and, dismissing protests by his staff, ordered an attack on Fort Vaux for 03.00 on 2 June. Inside the fort, Raynal had watched helplessly as the Germans overran his flank protection, and correctly surmised that a direct attack on the fort would not be long in coming from the now uncovered dead ground to the north-east. As the German preparatory barrage rose to a crescendo, with shells falling on the fort at a rate of 2,000 per hour, he therefore supervised the erection of sandbag barricades to protect nine separate

breaches in the fort's roof. The German attack came in as planned just before dawn on 2 June, and two battalions drawn from Infanterie Regiment 53 and Infanterie Regiment 158 from Infanterie Division 50 swept into the concrete moat where they came under mutually supporting machine gun fire from the north-west and north-east galleries. Attached pioneers knocked out the latter at around 05.00 when its machine gun jammed, but Captain Tabourot, the fort's deputy commander, held the interlopers back single-handed until mortally wounded by a grenade splinter. A Flammenwerfer attack on the north-west gallery silenced the machine guns therein long enough for a platoon-sized group from Infanterie Regiment 158 under Lieutenant Rackow to reach the fort glacis; they were then cut off when the machine guns came back into action. Repeated attempts to silence the gallery failed until the Germans discovered a sandbag-plugged breach in the roof of the corridor linking the gallery to the fort proper. Raynal then withdrew his men from the gallery before they could be cut off and set others to work erecting sandbag barriers to seal off both corridors.

By 16.00 the Germans were in possession of the whole fort super-structure, under command of Lieutenant Rackow. An attempt to penetrate into the fort from the north-east gallery succeeded in blowing in a steel door and sandbag barrier sealing off the corridor, but was halted by a hastily deployed machine gun. The Germans then concentrated on surrounding the fort during the hours of darkness, and renewed their underground efforts along both the gallery tunnels throughout 3 June. This consisted of rushing a series of sandbag barriers manned by lone French grenadiers, backed by a machine gun to protect men building the next barrier behind it. The fighting was hellish, with men struggling and clawing at one another in pitch blackness punctuated with the blinding flash of explosions that filled the cramped tunnels – which were only around three feet wide and four feet high in places – with smoke and fumes. The concrete walls magnified the concussion and chan-nelled the shrapnel and ricocheting small arms rounds. By midnight on 2 June the battalion from Infanterie Regiment 53 had lost all but one of its officers and that from Infanterie Regiment 158 hold-ing the surface had suffered severe losses to French artillery fire, to the extent that both battalions had to be replaced the following night.

The morning of 4 June saw a dawn relief attack by the 124th DI. Six waves of attackers pushed through shelling and machine gun fire to reach the western edge of the fort but were driven off with a bayonet charge by a fresh German battalion. The Germans then tried a new tack, attempting to smoke out Raynal's men by shooting Flammenwerfer into the fort from the surface. This filled the interior with choking black smoke and drove the men manning the barricades back in panic. The situation was saved by Lieutenant Girard who ran back up the north-west corridor as the flames died down and reached an abandoned machine gun in the nick of time. Despite suffering several wounds he held on until reinforcements arrived before succumbing to the effects of the smoke. The new tactic failed in an attack on the hitherto unmolested gallery at the south-west corner of the moat, where the defenders killed all the Flammenwerfer operators before they could carry out their attack. The weapons were promptly appropriated in a swift sally by the gallery garrison, who then used them to keep the ditch clear of further German interlopers.

The day's fighting gained the Germans twenty-five yards of the north-west tunnel that included the entrance to one of the fort's three observation domes, and inflicted twenty-five badly burned casualties on the French defenders. Raynal wrote a brief report informing his superiors that the fort was holding out despite attacks with gas and dangerous fumes, that relief was imperative, that Fort Souville was not responding to his signal lamp and that the bearer of the report was his last pigeon. The latter, Carrier Pigeon No.787-15, had been affected by the fumes and returned to the fort several times before flying off, then expired after delivering its message. It became the only pigeon to be awarded a posthumous *Légion d'Honneur* for its dedication to duty, and was preserved for posterity with the aid of a taxidermist.

The arrival of Carrier Pigeon No.787-15 prompted a supportive lamp signal from Fort Souville, which had assumed Vaux had fallen into German hands. This morale boost was swiftly dissipated in the afternoon of 4 June when Raynal was informed that the fort's water cistern was all but empty. Water supply problems had been identified in March 1916 but nothing had been done, and the cistern was apparently less than half full when Raynal assumed command. The defenders thus had thirst added to their travails, as Raynal was obliged to eke out the remaining supply by reducing the water ration to a quarter of a pint per man per day. He also despatched nineteen-year-old Officer Cadet Buffet to scout a route through the surrounding Germans after dark, so that the number of personnel in the fort could be reduced. Most appear to have been killed or captured en route, as only Buffet and eight others are reported to have reached the safety of Fort Tavannes, a mile and a half to the south.

33 The moat surrounding Fort Vaux. Note the rubble and masonry from the German bombardment. The Germans started a concerted attack on the fort on 1 June with a preparatory barrage that reached a rate of 2,000 shells per hour beginning in the late evening of that day, and German troops overran the fort superstructure in the early morning of 2 June. The fort, commanded by Major Sylvain-Eugene Raynal, finally surrendered on 7 June after an epic siege that cost the Germans 2,742 casualties.

34 The south-west side of Fort Vaux. Contrast this with the previous photograph taken before the German capture of the fort.

The Germans opened 5 June by blowing a large breach in the fort's south-west Casemate de Bourges with a buried mine at dawn. A follow-up flame attack literally backfired when a gust of air from within the fort blew the flames back onto the Flammenwerfer operators, which gave sufficient time for the gallant Lieutenant Girard to lead yet another successful riposte with grenades; Girard was wounded again in the process. Further German attempts to dig mine shafts were stymied by calling in shellfire from Fort Souville via signal lamp, but this tenuous link was removed in the afternoon when a German shell destroyed the signal station. An attempt to re-establish contact with a jury-rigged lamp later in the day drew no response, and morale was reduced yet again by further German gains along the north-east corridor. This cut off the fort garrison from their last latrine, thereby imposing further difficulty and indignity on the hard-pressed defenders. The morale pendulum swung up again with the return of Officer Cadet Buffet after dark, wearing a shiny new medal presented by Nivelle himself and bearing word of a bat-talion-strength relief attack scheduled for 02.00 on 6 June. Raynal and his men thought the job required more than a single battalion, and their pessimistic assessment proved all too accurate. The French preparatory barrage overshot the fort, and the attackers got only close enough to the fort for the disappointed defenders to witness the last of them being wiped out by German machine guns.

The failure of the relief attack plunged morale in the fort to new depths, and events through 6 June compounded the damage. The defend-ers rebuffed more German attacks, but repeated signals to Fort Souville went unacknowledged and a large-calibre German shell brought down a section of roof in the fort's main corridor. Thirst reduced the defenders to licking condensation from the concrete walls, and some resorted to drinking their own urine. The plight of the wounded, many of whom were severely burned and all of whom had gone without more than basic treatment for days, was the worst of all. By nightfall Raynal had decided enough was enough. He therefore flashed a final signal to Fort Souville at 03.30 on 7 June, and despatched one of his officers to the German-held barricade in the north-west corridor with a white flag. A delegation of German officers were then escorted to Raynal's command post through a hastily formed French honour guard, where they were presented with the ornate bronze key to the fort.

The garrison, which still included the by now somewhat bedraggled spaniel, were then evacuated and bemused their captors by breaking ranks to slurp the foul water from the first shell crater they happened upon. In a scene reminiscent of the nineteenth century, Raynal was taken to 5th Army HQ at Stenay on 8 June, where the Crown Prince presented him with a captured French officer's sword to replace his own, lost somewhere inside Fort Vaux. The German magnanimity toward their prisoners was highly creditable given the damage they had inflicted. The four German battalions involved in the attack on Fort Vaux lost a total of 2,742 officers and men, while the defenders lost twenty dead and around a hundred wounded.[70] The tale did not end quite there, however. Nivelle had organised another relief attack for 8 June, using North African troops from the 2nd Régiment de Zouaves and the *Régiment d'Infanterie Coloniale du Maroc*. Not only was this too late, but the attack ran headlong into a push south by Infanterie Division 50 to take advantage of the fall of Fort Vaux. The Zouaves were virtually annihilated by the German barrage as they left their trenches. The Moroccans, under the mistaken belief that the fort was still in French hands, pushed on through the German shelling and machine gun fire and actually reached the fort before being mown down by the new German garrison. An appalled Pétain then intervened and forbade Nivelle to make any further attempts to retake Fort Vaux.

The capture of Fort Vaux opened the way for a concerted German push to secure the last obstacles barring the way to Verdun. This was the ridge dominated by Fort Souville, after which there was only Fort Belleville and Fort St. Michel between them and Verdun, and those works could easily be outflanked if Souville were taken. It was the eastern end of this push, aimed toward Fort Tavannes, that subsumed the final attempt to relieve the fort by the 2nd Régiment de Zouaves and the *Régiment d'Infanterie Coloniale du Maroc* on 8 June. However, the main focus of the German assault was two and a half miles west of Vaux. The outer cordon of French fortifications stretched south-west from Fort Douaumont along the Côte de Thiaumont and Côte de Froideterre, a long interlinked ridge running down to the Meuse. It consisted of two works, the *Ouvrage de Froideterre* at the western end, two hardened *Postes de Commande* (command posts) converted into defence works known as PC118 and PC119, and, roughly midway between the latter and Fort Douaumont, the *Ouvrage de Thiaumont*. The latter was the key to any assault on Fort Souville. It blocked the approach to a spine of high ground running south-east straddled by the village of Fleury, which linked the Côte de Froideterre to the height dominated by Fort Souville.

The German attack on 8 June was therefore focussed on the *Ouvrage de Thiaumont*, and was preceded by an all-night artillery bombardment that inflicted severe casualties on the hapless French defenders. The 347th RI, which stood squarely in the German line of advance, was reduced to 356 men by the time the German infantry began to advance at dawn on 8 June. The latter quickly overran the

35 The *Ouvrage* de Thiaumont and access trench in May 1916, before the German offensive of early June.

Ouvrage de Thiaumont but were driven out by fierce French counter-attack, the first of fourteen occasions on which the fortification changed hands during the battle. Thereafter, the German attack made steady, if slow, progress, in part due to dogged French resistance and in part to the weather; the five days after 7 June were marked by heavy rain. Nonetheless, the German advance increased daily in intensity, to the extent that by 11 June Pétain reported to Joffre that the Germans had attained an artillery superiority of two to one.

The French disadvantage was exacerbated because they were running short of artillery observation posts as their line was pushed inexorably back, leading to a marked reduction in accuracy and a consequent rise in misdirected barrages falling on friendly troops. Balloon observation was also risky if not impossible, as the Germans had re-established air superiority over the battlefield. The period 8–12 June was thus the most severe crisis faced by the French at Verdun since 25 February. As in 1914, they were rescued from disaster by the Russians. On 4 June the latter launched the Brusilov Offensive against the Austro-Hungarian front in Galicia, which promptly collapsed with the loss of 400,000 prisoners. Four days later the Austro-Hungarian commander-in-chief, General Count Conrad von Hotzendorf, was obliged to call on Falkenhayn for help, a bitter task given that the two men loathed one another. Falkenhayn was thus obliged to send three divisions to the east to shore up the

Austro-Hungarians, and the Crown Prince was ordered to suspend the attack toward Fort Souville. The fighting thus died away with the French still in possession of the *Ouvrage de Thiaumont*. The German pause allowed the French to bring up reinforcements and shore up their battered defences.

The respite came not a moment too soon for the French, for by 12 June the reserve on the east bank of the Meuse had been reduced to a single infantry brigade. More seriously, the fighting provoked additional and disquieting examples of *défaillance* among the French units involved. Joffre's abolition of the noria system obliged French infantry formations to return to the front line more frequently and for longer than hitherto; by June 1916 French divisions were losing an average of 4,000 men every time they went into the line. The GQG representative to 2nd Army HQ noted the deleterious results of all this. Men from the 12th Corps responded to orders to return to the front with a sit-down strike, elements of the 64th RI reacted in a similar manner to their orders, and fifty men from the 140th RI were court-martialled for refusing point blank to re-enter the trenches. Perhaps typically, the GQG officer also complained that they had been treated too leniently for the gravity of their offence.[71] The German attack on 8 June cast the problem in even sharper relief. A battalion of the 291st RI near the *Ouvrage de Thiaumont* surrendered virtually intact. More seriously, the survivors of the 347th RI, which lost eighty per cent of its strength in the bombardment, were led back to barracks by their ranking surviving officer, a Lieutenant Herduin, after repeated requests for reinforcement had gone unanswered and a planned relief failed to materialise.

36 The badly damaged remains of the *Ouvrage de Thiaumont* after it was finally overrun and secured by the Germans on 23 June 1916.

In this instance the response of the French military hierarchy was far from lenient. Despite their exemplary records Lieutenant Herduin and another officer, Second Lieutenant Milan, were condemned to death for abandoning their post and were executed. The story provoked an outcry when revealed by Herduin's widow after the war, and both men were officially exonerated in 1926.[72] To reinforce the point at the time punishment was extended to the 291st and 347th RI collectively, both regiments being disbanded and their regimental colours returned to their respective depots in disgrace.

The attack to secure Fort Souville was scheduled to re-commence on 23 June 1916. Crown Prince Wilhelm spent the hiatus renewing his attempts to get Gericht terminated, but he was thwarted again by von Knobelsdorf and the Kaiser. The former had assembled 30,000 men, including a complete corps of elite Alpine troops under General Krafft von Dellmensingen. The attack itself was to be another two-stage affair, concentrating initially on securing the *Ouvrage de Thiaumont* and Fleury. Assigned to a three-mile frontage, the attack was to be the penultimate German effort to reach Verdun, and enjoyed a higher density of men per yard of frontage than the initial attack in February or on 8 June. Optimism was running so high that von Knobelsdorf went so far as to invite the Kaiser to the 5th Army's HQ at Stenay to witness the triumph, and ordered up the regimental bands and colours of the units involved for the anticipated victory parade. In part, the optimism was due to the fact that the attack was also to involve a new and particularly deadly secret weapon. German chemists had formulated a phosgene gas specifically to defeat French issue respirators, and the plan was to saturate the French artillery positions with shells containing the new gas, nicknamed Green Cross gas after the markings painted on the shells, before the attack commenced. Phosgene was an especially deadly substance that killed anything it came into contact with, including insects and plants, and was particularly insidious because its effects were not immediately apparent to the victim. By the time they did appear irreversible harm had been inflicted on the respiratory system, and the victim drowned on fluid produced by his damaged lungs.

The preparatory bombardment began with the firing of 116,000 Green Cross shells against the French artillery positions and conventional shells on the French front-line positions in the late evening of 22 June.[73] By dawn on 23 June the French artillery had been largely suppressed, and the gas had also caused chaos among the horse-drawn transport maintaining the flow of ammunition and food to the front line. The barrage switched back to high explosive three hours before dawn, when the German infantry left their trenches and pressed

37 The *Ouvrage de Froideterre*, two kilometres south-west of Thiaumont. Froideterre stood firm against the German offensive of 23 June 1916 and remained in French hands.

forward in the densest formations yet seen in the battle. The heaviest blow fell on the junction between the 129th DI and 130th DI, which were already demoralised by the barrage and lack of artillery support, water and ammunition. The *Ouvrage de Froideterre* was encircled and bypassed, the German troops pressing on down the reverse slope running south from the Ouvrage into the Ravine des Vignes to besiege a French underground command post nicknamed the *Quatre Cheminées* (four chimneys) after its four domed ventilation shafts. The shelter housed HQ units for four different French units, who were relieved by a counter-attack by the 114th BCP.

The main effort was directed against the *Ouvrage de Thiaumont*, which was swiftly overrun by the Bavarian Leib Regiment and Jäger Regiment 2 from von Dellmensingen's Alpine Corps. They were assisted by another sign of failing French morale, with a large proportion of the 121st BCP surrendering en masse. By 08.15 German troops were advancing into Fleury, almost a mile from their start line, although the French troops holding the village put up a dogged resistance and by the afternoon they were being supported by resurgent French artillery. In all the Leib Regiment had lost over 500 men by the afternoon, but they were also blindly lofting extreme-range machine gun fire over the Côte de Belleville into the streets of Verdun. By midnight Fleury was in their hands and a defence line had been established along the railway embankment running south-west from the village. Unfortunately this was in full view of French artillery observers, who directed fire onto the slightest sign of German activity.

The day's fighting cost the French around 13,000 casualties and an additional 4,000 taken prisoner, and it severely unsettled the

38a and b The German attack of 23 June 1916 carried their advance to the village of Fleury, half way along a spine of high ground linking the Thiaumont–Froideterre Ridge with the last high ground before Verdun. The Germans captured Fleury on 24 June 1916, and held it against eight separate French counter-attacks between 24 and 30 June.

French command. By the end of the day the Governor of Verdun was supervising the digging of trenches in the town proper in preparation for a last-ditch defence. According to the subsequent legend, Joffre and Nivelle prevented a rattled Pétain from evacuating the east bank of the Meuse, a view supported by Nivelle's famous order of the day which included the immortal line sometimes attributed to Pétain, '*Ils ne passeront pas!*' (They shall not pass!).[74] The charge against Pétain was based largely on a telephone exchange between him and de Castelnau in the afternoon of 23 June. However, Pétain had only been alerting GQG to the ramifications of a continuing German advance, while the supposedly resolute Nivelle was actually evacuating guns from the area of Bras and Froideterre. At the same time the allegedly unflappable Joffre was sufficiently concerned to redirect four divisions from his jealously guarded hoard for the upcoming Somme offensive to Verdun.

In the event, this buck-passing was unnecessary because although it was not apparent from the French side, the German attack had failed. This was partly because the attack frontage was too narrow to permit a clean breakthrough, and despite von Knobelsdorf's best efforts 5th Army lacked the reserves that would have permitted a resumption of the attack on 24 June. The three divisions sent east by Falkenhayn to assist their Austro-Hungarian allies might thus have made all the difference. The stock of phosgene gas shells had run down – there were insufficient available to cover anything more than the central sector of the attack frontage – and in any case the Green Cross gas had not performed as advertised. The French suffered only 1,600 gas casualties as their issue respirator proved less susceptible than expected, and the switch to conventional shells three hours or more before the infantry attack began allowed the French artillery to recover by the afternoon. The tendency for phosgene to pool in hollows also minimised the effect on French artillery emplaced on high ground. This was particularly the case with the Damloup Battery, sometimes referred to as the High Battery due to its 342-metre elevation, a hardened artillery position south-east of Fort Vaux with a clear line of fire on Fleury and the approaches to Fort Souville.

In addition, the weather had taken a hand, for 23 June was one of the hottest days of the year. This was exacerbated by the physical state of the battlefield, which the constant shelling had by this point ploughed into a cratered, milky brown desert bereft of foliage or shade. Adequate water supply for the men in the front line was thus vital, but as this was reliant on human bearers it was difficult if not impossible to achieve. Only twenty-eight of the ninety-five water bearers despatched to Fleury during the night of 23/24 June got through, for example,[75] and the German troops were thus physically incapable of continuing the attack. This did nothing to lessen the intensity of the fighting, however. Nivelle brought back Mangin, who had been sacked after the costly failure to retake Fort Douaumont at the end of May 1916, and placed him in charge of all operations on the east bank of the Meuse. He immediately launched a sustained effort to drive the Germans out of Fleury and retake Thiaumont. Between 24 and 30 June the French launched eight separate assaults, interspersed with German counter-attacks, and at the end of the period the only progress had been in lengthening the casualty list on both sides.

The focus of events then shifted north to the Somme, where the British New Army embarked on its own bleeding experiment on

1 July 1916. The first day of the long-awaited offensive cost the British 60,000 casualties, a third of them dead. By the time the battle ground to a halt in November, the British casualty toll had risen to 420,000, the Germans had lost an estimated 500,000 and the French formations that Joffre had so assiduously assembled had lost an additional 200,000 men. Back at Verdun, von Knobelsdorf was loath to admit that, with the events of 23 June, Gericht had failed. In fact, he remained convinced that victory was attainable with just one more effort, and he set about persuading Falkenhayn to grant him permission to launch it. The latter finally acquiesced, with the proviso that von Knobelsdorf attained his objective with whatever units he had to hand. The new attack was thus scheduled to begin on 9 July, and was to be a two-pronged affair again aimed at Fort Souville. One prong was to drive straight down the narrow spine of high ground running south from Fleury using the three divisions already ensconced there. As we have seen, these formations had been badly depleted in the late June fighting; Jäger Regiment 3, for example, had suffered 1,200 casualties.[76] The second prong was to approach Souville from the area of Fort Vaux to the east.

However, the eastern line of attack was blocked by the Damloup Battery, which consisted of a number of hardened gun pits and concrete bunkers defended by a reinforced infantry company. The task of capturing the battery was entrusted to Infanterie Division 50, the formation that had conquered Fort Vaux. The task was accomplished with an imaginative ruse involving a number of heavy-calibre Minenwerfers. These set a pattern of staging short but intense barrages on the Damloup Battery, during which the French defenders developed the habit of withdrawing to the safety of their bunkers. German assault troops crept close to the battery under cover of such a barrage in the early hours of 3 July, where they waited until the Minenwerfers began firing bombs without fuses at 02.00. They then swept forward and overran the battery before the defenders realised what was afoot, taking a hundred or more prisoner. Preparations for the main attack went ahead, although on 7 July the weather took a hand again and torrential rain prompted a two-day postponement. The rain was a mixed blessing for the German troops clinging to their improvised front line behind the railway embankment at Fleury, for while it alleviated their thirst, it also swiftly turned the shell-churned battlefield into a milky swamp that swallowed men and equipment. This was also poor preparation for troops who had already been exposed to unceasing French artillery fire for three days, which cost the lead battalion 120 men before the attack began. This had obvious consequences for morale, which were exacerbated by strict orders forbidding daylight movement, including rendering assistance to the wounded.

8

The Final German Effort: 10–12 July 1916

The bombardment for the attack began at midnight on 10 July. Green Cross gas again played an important part in the German fire plan, which had been amended to avoid repeating the mistakes of 23 June by continuing to drop gas shells onto the French artillery positions until the assault infantry were on the move. Ironically and perhaps typically, Falkenhayn had undergone another change of mind. He withdrew permission for the assault and ordered 5th Army to adopt a defensive posture, but in spite of the two-day postponement the order was issued too late to reach the German divisional HQs in time to stop the attack. Be that as it may, the eastern advance from the Damloup Battery by Jäger light infantrymen supported by Flammenwerfer teams surprised and routed the 217th RI, overrunning the regimental command post and capturing its commander. The French formation suffered over 1,300 casualties, and one battalion surrendered en masse after being encircled. This brought the German advance close to the entrance of the Tavannes Tunnel, which carried the single-track Verdun–Metz railway line for a kilometre and a half under the Côte de Belleville ridge. The French had been using the tunnel as a conduit for moving troops and supplies to the eastern end of the Verdun frontage since early in the battle. It had thus become home for a number of transport, supply, medical and signal units as well as a great number of stragglers seeking shelter from the incessant shelling. It is unclear whether the Germans appreciated the value or indeed existence of the tunnel, the seizure of which would have allowed them to bypass Fort Souville and the forts on the Côte de Belleville and provided a virtually unopposed route straight to Verdun. The fact that they do not appear to have made a serious effort to secure it suggests they did not. The French were understandably disinclined to take the chance and the German advance of 11 July prompted hasty arrangements for demolition.

The attack from Fleury initially fared less well. The French had issued an improved respirator that largely nullified the effects of the Green Cross gas and restricted gas casualties to a handful. The French artillery, demonstrating admirable restraint, thus held its fire until the German assault troops began to advance at dawn and then smothered the German front line with fire. This caught Jäger Regiment 3 and Infanterie Regiment 140 as they left the shelter of the battered railway embankment at Fleury. One battalion of the latter lost all its officers in a matter of minutes, and the commander of the former ordered his men to dig in and reported that any advance was impossible. Incredibly, the survivors reorganised themselves and pushed on regardless. The commander of the French 255th Brigade was killed when his command post was overrun, and some of his men were seen firing on their comrades who tried to surrender. By nightfall the Germans had penetrated 400 yards into the French front line toward Fort Souville, and had taken 2,400 prisoners.

The attack was resumed at dawn on 12 July and sparked confused fighting as troops clashed unexpectedly along the poorly defined front line. The German infantry were by now approaching exhaustion, and Falkenhayn's insistence that 5th Army carry out the attack without reinforcement meant there were no fresh troops to maintain the momentum of the advance. Nonetheless, in the late morning observers at von Dellmensingen's forward HQ noted a group of men atop Fort Souville waving a German flag. German artillery was immediately

39 French troops in a trench running through the remains of Fleury, pictured in October 1916, just after the village had been retaken. The Germans held Fleury from 24 June 1916 and launched one thrust of their final attack toward Verdun from the village on 10-12 July 1916; the consequent French counter-attacks between July and October literally erased Fleury from the map. Note the use of bricks and stonework from destroyed buildings to shore up the trench sides.

40a, b and c The final German attack
toward Verdun on 11–12 July 1916 was
a two-pronged affair, with one prong
being aimed toward Fort Tavannes.
As these pictures show, the German
bombardment devastated the woods
around the fort, and seriously damaged
the moat and interior courtyard of the
fort itself.

ordered to shell the area south of the fort to seal it off, but there were
no reserves available to send forward to complete the seizure. The men
waving the flag were in fact a stray group of thirty or so from Infanterie
Regiment 140, possibly commanded by an unknown ensign, who had
been driven forward by French artillery fire. Their flag waving was an
effort to attract reinforcements and presumably deflect the German
artillery fire falling on the fort. It took the French some time to react
and in the interim the German interlopers were able to see Verdun
basking in the summer haze less than two miles distant. Then a scratch
group made up from a variety of units sheltering inside the fort sallied
forth, led by a Lieutenant named Dupuy. This was a courageous move
in itself, for Dupuy had no idea how many intruders there actually were.
Several Germans were killed in the ensuing fight, ten were captured
and the remainder driven off.

Although it would not become apparent for some time, their
departure marked the high water mark of the German advance
toward Verdun, 139 days after Operation Gericht was launched,
for two days later the German 5th Army was ordered to suspend
operations at Verdun. Over that time both sides had fired a total of
37 million artillery shells, 22 million by the Germans alone, and
the battle had occupied the attention of forty-seven German divisions and seventy of the ninety-six French divisions assigned to the
Western Front. The disparity was due to Pétain's noria system which
spread the burden more equally across the French Army, as opposed

to the German system of leaving divisions in the line and continually topping them up with replacements. Even so, the French Army had paid a horrendous price. By 15 July 1916 the fighting at Verdun had cost the French Army almost 282,000 casualties, including between 65,000 and 70,000 dead, and a further 65,400 taken prisoner.[77]

Neither was this the final butcher's bill, for the cessation of *Gericht* did not bring the Verdun fighting to a stop. This was largely because the French had no way of knowing that the attack of 11–12 July was the final German effort, and the latter were still too close to their objective for comfort. Thus Mangin launched a series of counter-attacks which by 14 July had pushed the Germans back to their 11 July start line, and continued through July and into August 1916 on the transverse ridge straddled by Fleury and controlled by the *Ouvrage de Thiaumont*. The fighting for the converted command post PC119 was especially heavy, and in the process Fleury was reduced from a village with a population of around 500 to a brick-coloured smear in the finely churned soil. The only tangible relic recovered later was a silver chalice from the village church.[78] Eventually the cost of the often poorly co-ordinated French piecemeal counter-attacks became too heavy. On one occasion, for example, Pétain was moved to remonstrate with Mangin when a particularly badly mismanaged attack on Fleury caused heavy loss to the 37th DI. This had the required effect, and French activity east of the Meuse was toned down while a large-scale counter-offensive was organised.

There was little diminution by the French artillery in this period, however, a policy referred to as 'not burying the hatchet' by Mangin. The daily, routine losses thus continued, recorded under the chillingly dehumanised heading of 'wastage'. This tally received an unwelcome boost on 4 September when an accidental explosion in the Tavannes Tunnel, allegedly caused by a mule cargo of signal rockets catching fire, caused a chain reaction like that which had ripped through German-held Fort Douaumont on 8 May. The blast wiped out a brigade HQ and at least two companies of troops, and a coincidental German artillery barrage at the eastern end of the tunnel drove back survivors looking to flee the carnage. The ensuing fire burned so fiercely that it was impossible to enter the tunnel for three days, and investigators found piles of charred corpses gathered beneath the vertical ventilation shafts in the roof where men had sought escape. The final death toll was estimated to have been in the range of 500 men.[79]

The French counter-offensive was organised by Pétain, who approached the matter with his customary efficiency and attention to detail. The objective was to push the German line back to the Côte

41a and b The main target of the final German attack on 11–12 July 1916 was Fort Souville, which guarded the last ridge of high ground between the Germans and Verdun. Only a small party of German troops managed to reach the fort's glacis on 12 July, and they were driven off by a counter-attack by the fort's garrison. The picture of the fort's main gate was taken in September 1916, and the snowy view of the inner entrance in March 1917. Both views show the damage inflicted by several months of sustained German bombardment.

de Froideterre and recapture Fort Douaumont, and through August and September 1916 he assembled eight divisions to accomplish the task. The first wave of the attack consisted of the 38th, 74th and 177th DIs, with the *Régiment d'Infanterie Coloniale du Maroc* being assigned the task of securing Fort Douaumont. They were to be followed by a second wave of three divisions, supported by a reserve of two divisions. A replica of the attack frontage was constructed near Bar-le-Duc for the assault troops to train on, which included a full-size outline of Fort Douaumont. Other preparations included engaging a civilian engineer involved in constructing the Panama Canal to design and build a method of pumping water over the battlefield using a system of canvas pipes, and burying all telephone cables six feet deep to protect them from shellfire. The latter was especially important, for close co-ordination was a key point in the artillery fire plan drawn up by Nivelle, which included a rolling barrage that would advance at a rate of 100 metres every four minutes, between seventy-five and 150 metres in front of the advancing infantry. In all 650 guns and 150,000 tons of artillery ammunition were amassed to support the attack including two brand-new 400mm railway guns, the heaviest pieces yet deployed by the French Army.[80]

9

French Counter-offensives and Aftermath: October 1916–2005

The barrage began on 19 October 1916 and ceased on the afternoon of 22 October, prompting the Germans to launch their counter-bombardment in the belief that the French infantry attack had begun. In fact the pause was a ruse and the German artillery was promptly smothered by French counter-battery fire that knocked out 158 German batteries and damaged several more. The French bombardment then resumed. At around midday on 23 October the first 400mm round struck Fort Douaumont in tandem with a gas bombardment on the exits. The French railway guns were more powerful than the German 420mm pieces, and months of bombardment had weakened the fort's defences by stripping away most of the four metres of soil protecting the concrete carapace. The first round thus penetrated to the fort's upper level and burst in an infirmary, killing fifty wounded and medical personnel. The sixth round penetrated to the lower levels and sparked a sympathetic detonation in an ammunition store, which in turn began a fierce fire. Rounds continued to land every ten to fifteen minutes until darkness blocked effective spotting, by which time the fort's bakery and two casemates had been destroyed, and a section of the main corridor had been blocked by a roof collapse. The shells bursting inside the previously impervious fort caused an understandable panic and the fort commander, a Major Rosendahl, eventually ordered an evacuation apart from a handful of fire-fighters and two men in one of the outlying machine gun galleries who did not receive the word. At around 07.00 on 24 October a small group of artillery signallers under a Hauptmann Prollius wandered into the fort in dense fog. Finding the fires still burning but the fort essentially habitable, he despatched a runner to summon reinforcements. By then it was too late.

The French preparatory barrage ceased at dawn on 24 October, after firing 250,000 shells. The German artillery, wary of a second ruse, failed to respond for twelve minutes, by which time the French infantry, advancing behind their rolling barrage and assisted by the dense fog, were into the German front-line trenches in places. Fleury and the *Ouvrage de Thiaumont* were overrun in minutes, and eye-witness reports refer to no-man's-land being littered with packs dropped by their owners to allow them to move faster. The battalion from the *Régiment d'Infanterie Coloniale du Maroc* assigned to take Fort Douaumont, commanded by Major Nicolai, initially became disoriented in the gloom but was guided back on target when the fog lifted briefly. In an almost mirror image of events the previous 25 February, the unfortunate Captain Prollius and his handful of signallers were obliged to surrender the virtually unmanned fort. Douaumont was firmly in French hands by the late afternoon, when the fog lifted to reveal a party of Moroccan troops atop the fort in the weak autumn sunshine. An eyewitness likened the scene to a similar event at Austerlitz in 1805. By the end of the day the French had advanced three kilometres, a distance it had taken their German opponents four and a half months to achieve. In part, the French success was due to low German morale. The German units involved had been in the line since the beginning of the battle, and they were exhausted, undermanned and their equipment was largely worn out, with shells regularly dropping short onto German positions. Six thousand Germans were taken prisoner, many without a fight, some claiming to have had no food for six days.[81]

The French kept up the pressure. Fort Vaux was re-occupied on 2 November without a fight, after being abandoned by its German garrison. The next six weeks were taken up by preparations for another major French offensive. These included constructing eight-een miles of roadway and several miles of narrow-gauge railway to help move and supply the 760 artillery pieces slated to support the attack, which began on 15 December. Carried out on a six-mile frontage by four divisions, this attack pushed the Germans back almost to their 21 February start line and cost them over 11,000 prisoners and 115 guns. With the front line once again five miles from Verdun, the threat to the town was finally alleviated. A further attack on both sides of the Meuse on 20 August 1917 regained Côte 304, the Mort Homme, the Côte de l'Oie and the Bois d'Avocourt, push-ing the Germans back to their west bank start line on 6 March and losing them a further 9,500 prisoners.[82] The final major operation in the area began on 26 September 1918. Also straddling the Meuse, this was a multi-national affair, with the American Expeditionary

Force being responsible for the area west of the river. Lasting until the end of October, the attack gained an even bigger bag of German prisoners at some 20,000. On the east bank of the Meuse they finally recovered the Bois de Caures, where Colonel Driant and his valiant little band of light infantrymen from the 56th and 59th BCP had stood against the might of the German 17th Corps. Matters had thus finally turned full circle, after two years and eight months.

The recapture of the Bois de Caures in September–October 1918 may have brought the matter full circle, but the Battle of Verdun is commonly accepted to have extended between February and December 1916. Within those chronological parameters the battle cost a total of 681,000 casualties. The French lost 56,000 dead, 195,000 wounded and an additional 100,000 missing. The cost to the Germans was only marginally less, at 330,000 including 143,000 dead and missing.[83] For all this horrendous price in human life and suffering, Gericht failed to attain its overt objective, for the closest the Germans came to Verdun was the glacis of Fort Souville. Neither did Falkenhayn's covert experiment in deliberate attrition attain its objective. The French Army had certainly been bled but proved sufficiently resilient to absorb the punishment meted out by its opponent, albeit with a rising occurrence of incidents of défaillance. More pertinently, as the figures cited above show, the bleeding had turned into a mutual rather than one-way process, and the margin of difference that was hardly economic even if it had been otherwise acceptable.[84] This view was supported by an appalled Field Marshal Paul von Hindenburg and his chief of staff, General Erich Ludendorff, on visiting the Verdun battlefield after August 1916. Significantly, the former commented that 'Battles there [Verdun] exhausted our forces *like an open wound*' (author's italics). Ludendorff echoed his chief's view, commenting that the German losses had been simply too heavy to bear.[85]

The toll extracted by the Battle of Verdun was not restricted to the horrendous price in human life and limb, but also impacted on the reputations and subsequent careers of those who prosecuted it. Despite the failure of 11–12 July 1916, von Knobelsdorf remained convinced that Verdun could be reached with one more effort, and Falkenhayn appears to have been contemplating maintaining his bleeding experiment, albeit at a less intensive level. However, the Kaiser, finally disillusioned by the disjoint between Falkenhayn's repeated assurances of success and the reality, finally paid heed to his son. Von Knobelsdorf was thus reassigned to Russia on 23 August 1916, after which he faded from view. Falkenhayn was finally undone by the entry of Romania into the war on the Allied side four days

42 Fort Douaumont was retaken on 23 October 1916 by North African soldiers after a preparatory bombardment that used a quarter of a million shells. This picture shows men of the *Régiment d'Infanterie Coloniale du Maroc* sheltering in the moat of the fort on the afternoon of 23 October.

43 The rear aspect of Fort Douaumont, showing the damage inflicted by eight months of near constant bombardment. Contrast this with the pictures of the fort taken in January 1916. The back wall of a casemate, with firing slits, can be seen just right of centre.

later, in direct contradiction of his adamant insistence that such a development was impossible at that time. He resigned on 28 August and was replaced as Chief of the German General Staff by von Hindenburg, whose reaction on visiting the Verdun battlefield with Ludendorff has been cited above. Falkenhayn then at least partly rehabilitated himself with a highly successful campaign in Romania, and finished the war on attachment to the Turkish Army in Palestine. He died in April 1922, his health reportedly undermined by psychological problems; according to a relative Falkenhayn was unable to sleep because of his involvement in events at Verdun.[86]

On the other side of the line the combination of Verdun and the Somme did for Joffre, who was promoted out of the way in December 1916. He too sank into obscurity, spending over a decade preparing his memoirs before passing away in 1931. In this instance the replacement commander-in-chief proved to be worse than the original, as Nivelle was selected for largely political reasons over more competent candidates like Pétain or General Ferdinand Foch. Nivelle appears to have ignored or at least drastically underestimated the significance of the overt acts of défaillance that marked the closing stages of the fighting at Verdun. When President Poincaré visited Verdun in December 1916 to award decorations, for example, his car was stoned by poilus who heckled him with shouts of 'embusqué', a French military slang term for 'shirker'. Graffiti was noted on the main route from Verdun to the front line directing troops along the *Chemin de l'Abattoir* (path to the abattoir), and on 10 December a formation marching forward for the 15 December attack took to bleating like sheep.[87]

The straw that finally broke the camel's back was Nivelle's much vaunted offensive on the River Aisne against the Chemin des Dames ridge in April 1917. Despite his grandiose claims to have invented a winning formula, on this occasion the rolling barrage that had performed so well at Verdun in October and December 1916 failed to work its magic. This was partly because despite advice to the contrary Nivelle insisted on attacking a highly fortified section of the German line, and again because of unforgivably lax security; full details of the attack plan were published in the Paris press. The offensive began on 16 April, and within nine days the French Army had lost 30,000 dead, 100,000 wounded and 4,000 missing or taken prisoner.[88] Units began to refuse to obey orders to attack on 17 April and the mutiny then spread rapidly, ultimately affecting sixty-eight divisions to various degrees and involving around 40,000 men, and while the mutiny peaked in May and June 1917, incidents of indiscipline continued until January 1918. Pétain replaced Nivelle at the end of April, an embarrassing process in which Nivelle was forcibly ejected from his office while vociferously laying blame for the debacle on the Chemin des Dames on his subordinates, and Mangin in particular. Banished to North Africa, he died in 1924. Mangin went on to command an army group, performed well in the 1918 fighting and was placed in charge of the occupied Rhineland after the Armistice. He died in post in 1925, allegedly after being poisoned by German nationalists.

Pétain thus inherited the unenviable task of quelling the unrest, restoring order and rebuilding the Army's morale. He approached the task with his customary thoroughness, and 499 men were tried by court martial and sentenced to death for disciplinary offences. In the event, all but twenty-seven of the sentences were commuted, although that total does not include men summarily executed rather than court-martialled. The full price of restoring order has therefore yet to be established, and that will remain the case until the official documentation is released from the French government archives in 2017. The fact that this has been locked away from public scrutiny for a century reflects that the matter remains an extremely sensitive subject in France. In addition to the death sentences, 515 men were sent to prison for between five and fifteen years, with another 742 receiving sentences ranging from fifteen days and five years. A further 650 were sentenced to forced labour for between three years and life, and a further 1,438 were sentenced to communal labour for one or two years.[89] In some instances complete units were disbanded, their members being dispersed across the Army, and other units were suppressed and officially stripped of their colours as a mark of disgrace. Neither did the burden fall solely on the rank and file. Two generals and nine lieutenant-colonels were relieved of their commands for poor performance or incompetence.

Pétain rebuilt the Army's confidence by paying heed to the needs and welfare of the common poilu, in the same way he had restored the faith of the troops at Verdun in February 1916. He personally toured ninety divisions stationed along the Western Front, talking to the troops and listening to their complaints and grievances. In practical terms the solution was largely a matter of providing the poilus with arrangements and privileges that were considered routine provision in other contemporary armies. Thus for the first time since the conflict began French soldiers were given an official entitlement to leave every four months, the requisite road and rail transport and the right to appeal if leave was delayed or denied. Special rest centres were set up for troops withdrawn from the line, and regulations were enacted to ensure that they were actually allowed to rest, rather than being used as a convenient source of manual labour. The centres were also provided with field kitchens with properly trained cooks who ensured the troops were fed with fresh produce and especially green vegetables as a health measure. In addition, legislation was passed to spread the burden of conscription more equitably, and financial arrangements were put in place to assist the families of soldiers killed in action.

Pétain's measures were popular with poilu and public alike, and he was widely hailed as *Le médecin de l'Armée* (the Army's doctor).[90] His treatment restored the French Army's morale and effectiveness and thus enabled it to weather the German offensives at the beginning of 1918, and to perform its own counterstrokes that ultimately obliged the latter to accept the Armistice in November 1918. Thereafter Pétain served as Inspector General of the Army and Minister of War, and was called on to step into the breach in the summer of 1940, taking on the thankless task of heading the collaborationist Vichy regime after the French defeat. On this occasion his efforts were less well received after the event, and he fell victim to the French predilection for scapegoating. Field Marshal Philippe Pétain was tried and sentenced to death for treason in August 1945, the sentence being commuted to life imprisonment in view of his age. He died in 1951, aged ninety-five, on the Île d'Yeu off the French Atlantic coast where he had been imprisoned, and is interred in a small military cemetery on the island. His wish to be buried among his soldiers at Verdun, where a plot has been reserved in the cemetery outside the huge Ossuary atop the Thiaumont Ridge, has thus far been denied by successive French governments.

However, the battle had the greatest and longest lasting impact on the ground over which it was fought. On the west side of the River Meuse, the villages like Avocourt and Chattancourt destroyed in the fighting between March and May 1916 were rebuilt and most of the arable land surrounding Côte 304 and the Mort Homme was returned to its former use. The heights themselves defied reha-bilitation, however, and were finally sown with conifer trees in the 1930s; they were witness to brief but bitter fighting in the German breakout from the Ardennes in 1940. Both summits are marked with memorials, the Mort Homme with a macabre representation of Death rising from the earth cradling a furled flag, mounted on a plinth inscribed *Ils n'ont pas passé* (They did not pass). Côte 304 has a tall, imposing column bearing names of the units that fought there along with a simple dedication to the 10,000 men who remain in the hill. Beyond the memorials, however, signs of the battle remain clearly evident. Even a cursory visual inspection of the ground under the conifer canopy still reveals a moonscape of shell craters and

partially demolished trenches, their outlines blanketed but hardly
altered by nearly a century's worth of pine needles and the occasional
selective timber harvesting. The latter's heavy machinery routinely
throws up shrapnel, unexploded ordnance and even human remains.
The ordnance can often be seen casually piled for the attention of
French Army bomb disposal teams. Writing in 1962, Alistair Horne
noted a paucity of visitors to the west bank heights and referred
to them as 'one of the eeriest placers in this world… [where a]
grown man will not willingly repeat the experience of getting lost
in the labyrinth of firecuts that crisscross the deserted plantations'.[92]
Having visited both sites on a number of occasions more recently,
the present author would largely concur with this verdict.

Be that as it may, the most indelible evidence of the battle can be
found on the east bank of the Meuse. There the ground was poisoned even more badly by the combination of poison gas, chemical
explosive and corrupted human and animal flesh, and the topsoil
itself was scorched away by the constant artillery fire. Consequently,
the battlefield there resolutely resisted all attempts to turn it back
to arable usage. Even if that were not the case, the population of
the villages and hamlets in the area where the fighting was heaviest
were dispersed as refugees, and there was little for them to return
to had they been so inclined. Nine villages there were totally erased,
traceable only as a differently coloured smear in the churned earth or
through the odd brick or shards of roof tile. Eight of the disappeared
villages are marked with marker stones. The exception is Fleury,
which, chosen as an overall memorial due to its central location,
still boasts a symbolic mayor and has had its street plan laid out for
posterity as a series of woodland paths.

Memorials abound in what the French refer to as the Coeur du
Champ de Bataille (the heart of the battlefield). The high point
of the German advance is marked with a wounded lion, and the
site of Fleury railway station is occupied by a two-storey memorial
museum that boasts a life-size diorama of a section of the battlefield.
Most impressive of all is the huge Ossuary, almost two hundred yards
in length, constructed atop the Thiaumont Ridge. Semi-cylindrical
in shape and surmounted by a tower designed to represent an artillery shell, the Ossuary contains the remains of 130,000 unidentified
French soldiers gathered from across the battlefield; a further 15,000
identified men are interred the *Cimetière National* to its front. The
memorials exist cheek by jowl with more immediate evidence of the
fighting. West of the Ossuary the battered remains of the *Ouvrage de
Thiaumont* and PC 118 and 119 can be seen just off the minor road
running down to the Meuse. The intact *Ouvrage de Froideterre* has

gained a car park, an information board and benches for visitors, as has the *Quatre Cheminées* shelter with its horizon-bleu painted ventilation covers across the road to the south.

The courtyard of Fort Douaumont has also been turned into a car park, and visitors can follow rough footpaths that run along the rim of craters, between the turrets and observation domes on the glacis and along the defensive ditches. Fort Vaux has received similar treatment, and the back wall of the fort boasts large memorial plaques to Major Raynal and his most celebrated subordinate, *Légion d'Honneur* winner Carrier Pigeon No.787-15, souvenir brass replicas of whom can be purchased from a small shop within. For a small fee visitors can also prowl the dank interior corridors of both forts and marvel at the courage and fortitude of men like Captain Tabourot and Lieutenant Girard who endured, fought and in many instances died in the fumes and flame-torn darkness.

The remains of other, less well preserved forts can also be found nestling quietly in the greenery. The entrance to Fort Souville, complete with signs warning the unwary of the dangers of venturing within, can be found just off a wide bridle path, and the badly battered remains of Fort Tavannes lie a few yards beyond another sign marking the boundary of a French military reservation. A good deal of the battlefield is still used by the French Army as a training area. Fort Douaumont overlooks an anti-tank firing range, for example, and it is not uncommon to come across the blue plastic remains of training grenades, discarded ration cans and hastily filled-in slit trenches alongside the woodland trails that criss-cross the battlefield. It can be a jarring experience to unexpectedly come face to face with groups of modern French soldiers, bristling with weapons and field radios, practising their craft on the ground where so many of their forebears died. And everywhere off the metalled roads and unmade tracks are the craters and trenches, softened only slightly by light underbrush and decades of deadfall, undulating and snaking away in all directions like the surface of a petrified sea.

In 1987, following a formal reconciliatory meeting on the battlefield between the French President and German Chancellor three years earlier, the United Nations bestowed the title of World Capital of Peace, Freedom and Human Rights on Verdun. It is interesting to speculate on what the poilus who fought there in 1916 would have made of such a development. Be that as it may, this attempt to utilise Verdun's now not quite so recent heritage as an awful exemplar of the horrific reality of modern industrialised warfare is commendable. Only time will tell whether it has the desired result, or whether future generations will again ignore the lessons of history.

PART 2

Verdun: Battlefield Guide

1 The twin-towered *Porte Chaussée* gateway to Verdun. Constructed in 1380, this was originally set into the medieval rampart that encircled the town. The white van in the centre of the picture is just coming off the *Pont Chaussée* bridge across the River Meuse.

2 The southern end of the *Quai de Londres*.

10

Reaching Verdun

The most direct route to Verdun from Calais is via the French motorway or Autoroute system. At 388 kilometres (242 miles), the journey can be done comfortably within four hours. (Note: all distances below are given primarily in kilometres to avoid confusion with local road signage.) Also to avoid confusion, note that French motorways have two designations, their Autoroute (A) number and a Euro (E) number that ties them into the wider European road network. Consequently, many major non-motorway roads also have E-numbers. Note also that the Autoroute is a toll system, although the stretches around major cities are free because they also serve as the local ring roads. The toll charges are not especially high, and the toll sections are signposted as péage well in advance. Using them usually involves taking a ticket from an automated dispenser, which has to be presented at a booth for payment when leaving the Autoroute. Be warned that the payment system logs the entrance and exit time, and arriving at the exit before the time necessary to cover the section at or below the applicable speed limit can end with an on-the-spot speeding fine from the police.

The A16/E402 runs straight into the ferry and hovercraft terminal at Calais. Leave Calais on this road, and follow the signs onto the A26/E15 for St Omer *péage* – Paris *péage*. Remain on the A26/E15 for the 265km (165 miles) to Reims. There follow the signs for Metz onto the A4/E50 and remain on that road for the 126km (78 miles) to junction 30. Leave the A4/E50 there and follow the signs for Verdun onto the N35 (N roads are the equivalent to British A roads). The N35 is part of the *Voie Sacrée* (Sacred Way), the road linking Verdun to Bar-le-Duc. After 4km (2 ½ miles) the N35 runs into a T junction. Turn right onto the N3 toward Verdun, which lies 8km (5 miles) further on.

A longer but more scenic route can be found by following the above onto the A26/E15. Leave the latter after 130km (82 miles) at junction 8, and follow the D939 for 10km (7 miles) toward Cambrai. From Cambrai follow the N43/E44 for 150km (94 miles) through Le Cateau, where the British Expeditionary Force fought a desperate rearguard action on 26 August 1914, Le Nouvion-en-Thiérache, La Capelle, Hirson and Mon Idée to Charleville-Mézières. From there head toward Sedan on the same road, although the 30 kilometre (19 mile) stretch immediately after Charleville is a motorway, the A203/E44. In Sedan go right on to the D964, which runs south for 65km (42 miles) along the River Meuse through Stenay, Dun and into Verdun from the north.

Verdun is well served for accommodation. The town itself contains eleven hotels, with a further eight in the immediate vicinity. These run from 3-star to bed-and-breakfast establishments, with prices ranging from 205 to 28 euros. There is also an excellent campsite with facilities including a swimming pool on the southern outskirts, a mere ten-minute walk or so from the town centre. Full details of all these establishments, complete in most instances with telephone and email contact details, can be found on the Verdun Tourist Board website, the link for which is included in the bibliography at the end of this book.

3 The northern end of the *Quai de Londres*, marked by the white temporary roofing running left behind the trees from the centre of the picture. The dark stairway and tapering tower in the centre of the picture is the Victory Monument on the Rue Mazel. The top of the monument is a cloaked Gallic warrior resting on his sword pommel, and the doorway to the crypt housing the Golden Book containing the names of all those decorated in the fighting for Verdun can be seen at the base.

4 Monument to the Fallen of Verdun, sometimes referred to as the Monument to the Children of Verdun. Located just across the Meuse from the *Porte Chaussée*, the memorial represents the five French Army corps that fought at Verdun in 1916.

5 Monument to General Maurice Sarrail, who distinguished himself whilst commanding the French 3rd Army in the Ardennes fighting north of Verdun in 1914. The monument is located opposite the Monument to the Fallen.

6 The terminus of the *Voie Sacrée* in Verdun. To the left one of the special stones that mark the every kilometre of the route between Verdun and Bar-le-Duc can be seen, topped with a cast metal Adrian helmet. The pillar on the right marks the *Voie de la Liberté*, the route followed by the French 2nd Armoured Division in the liberation of France in 1944. The route runs for 1,446 kilometres from St Mère Église in Normandy to Strasbourg on the River Rhine.

7a and b The 'Ghosts' monument to the dead and missing of the 106th *Régiment d'Infanterie* lost in the fighting on the Les Éparges ridge on 17–19 February 1915. The monument was inspired by Maurice Genevoix's novel *Ceux de '14* (Those of '14), which was based on his service as a second lieutenant with the 106th *Régiment d'Infanterie*.

8a and b The monument to the French dead at Point X, the eastern high point of the Les Éparges ridge, seen through the grove of trees linking it to the car park and in close-up. The plaques are memorials to individuals and units dedicated by relatives and comrades.

9a and b Craters and trenches on either side of the path to the Point X monument.

10 The view over the Woëvre Plain looking east from Point X.

11 A collapsed German bunker at the bottom of the Les Éparges ridge below Point X.

Verdun

Verdun contains a variety of attractions for the visitor, not all of which are connected to the events of 1916–18. The town is dominated by the seventeenth-century Vauban Citadel and the Notre Dame Cathedral, which overlook it from the steep bluff that rises from the River Meuse. The latter is flanked by the eighteenth-century Bishop's Palace, and the oldest surviving gate into the town, the twelfth-century Porte Châtel, stands nearby. The St. Vanne Tower, the only remains of the cathedral's twelfth-century predecessor, stands inside the Vauban Citadel, while the main bridge across the Meuse is guarded by the *Porte Chaussée*, an imposing twin-towered gateway constructed in 1380 to control the *Pont Chaussée* bridge across the River Meuse. The town contains numerous cafes and restaurants, many of which line the *Quai de Londres* (London Quay), a paved plaza that runs along the Meuse from the *Pont Chaussée* and provides a most agreeable location for an outdoor evening meal or drink.

Just across the bridge from the *Pont Chaussée* gateway stands the Monument to the Fallen of Verdun, sometimes referred to as the Monument to the Children of Verdun, a larger-than-life relief representation of five French soldiers standing shoulder to shoulder, flanked by public gardens. The figures represent the five French Army corps that fought at Verdun in 1916, and the monument also features a memorial plaque dedicated to General Charles Mangin, who commanded the 5th *Division d'Infanterie* and later the entire French effort east of the River Meuse. Even more impressive is the Victory monument located on the Rue Mazel, Verdun's main shopping street which runs parallel and just back from the Meuse. Inaugurated in 1929 and standing atop a wide stairway, the monument consists of a rectangular tower topped by a cloaked Gallic warrior resting on his sword pommel, flanked with Russian cannon captured during the Crimean War. A crypt in the base of the tower houses the huge and ornate Golden Book containing the names of all those decorated in the fighting for Verdun. The crypt also plays a part in the annual Armistice Day commemorations, when it houses a torch lit at the Arc de Triomphe in Paris and a guard of honour for the eleven days leading up to 11 November.

There are also more tangible reminders of the events of 1916. Shrapnel damage is clearly evident on many older buildings, especially along the *Rue de Rû* (Brook Road) which runs west past the Citadel toward the *Porte Neuve* (New Gate), also known as the *Porte du Secours*. This part of the town remains virtually unchanged from the time of the battle, and it is not difficult to visualise the desperate scenes that accompanied the hasty evacuation of civilians from the town in the opening stages of the battle in February 1916. The novelist Henry Bordeaux, who served as a staff officer and became the semi-official historian of the battle, witnessed:

> women carrying babies or dragging along little children whose legs were giving way, wagons piled with mattresses and furniture. People had taken what they could, at random. Two old folk, husband and wife, side by side, were panting horribly and in the cold air their breath hung around them like a halo… Dogs followed the procession, tails down.[1]

The aftermath of the evacuation and the shelling which had prompted it was graphically described by a British war correspondent who visited Verdun at the beginning of March 1916:

> I have just been walking down the main street. Everywhere there is silence except for the crashing of the big shells and the sound of splinters falling on roofs… It was in the Rue Mazel that I met one of the three civilians of Verdun. He was contemplating the view from his door with a contented smile and looked at me with supreme contempt when I scuttled for cover at a particularly loud explosion. 'You are taking refuge on the wrongside [sic] of the road', he remarked mildly. 'The left is the side to escape from the splinters, since that is the side from which the Boches are firing. Anyway it is no use ducking, since by the time you have heard the shell the danger is over.'[2]

The *Rue de Rû* becomes the *Avenue de 5éme* RAP as it runs toward the *Porte Neuve*, and houses the entrance to the *Citadelle Souterraine* (Underground Citadel). This is a warren of passages and chambers underneath the Vauban citadel, which was employed as a shelter, barracks, HQ, cookhouse and supply depot all rolled into one during the battle. It was a staging post for units moving up to the line along

12 The steps leading up to the summit of the *Butte de Vauquois*, flanked by two French trench mortars.

13 The monument *Aux morts de la 40ᵉ DI* (To the dead of the 40th *Division d'Infanterie*) on the peak of the Mort Homme. The plaques on the plinth are memorials to individuals and units dedicated by relatives and comrades.

14 *Du Squelette* (Skeleton), monument to the dead of the 69th *Division d'Infanterie*. Although difficult to see at this angle, the plinth is inscribed *Ils n'ont pas passé* (They did not pass).

15 Memorial to the 173rd *Régiment d'Infanterie* at the junction of the D38 and D18 leading to Côte 304.

the *Voie Sacrée* (Sacred Way) from Bar-le-Duc, as described by an officer from the 106th *Régiment d'Infanterie*:

> We spend the day in the Citadel waiting. The guns fire ceaselessly. Huge shells (380s–420s) crash down on Verdun causing serious damage. I walk as far as the town: it's in ruins and deserted. One can't stay outside for long as shells are dropping everywhere. The Citadel is a real underground town, with narrow-gauge railway, dormitories, and rooms of every type; it's safe here, but very gloomy.[3]

This was echoed more graphically by Lieutenant René Arnaud of the 337th *Régiment d'Infanterie*:

> A bridge over a railway line, a road running between mist-laden meadows, zig-zagging alongside the river. Suddenly an enormous dark wall, flights of steps, muffled shouts, and the warm odour of cabbage, mouldy bread and creosol. I went down a long vaulted gallery through which passed tip-up trucks drawn by mules, making a deafening din. Doors opened on to typists' offices, engine rooms, and bakeries smelling of warm bread. Then, in the weak electric light, I passed through hall after hall filled with soldiers, some of them changing their clothes after the march for fear of catching a cold – for great danger did not make them forget the little ones – others eating ravenously from their mess tins and drinking out of their flasks. All these casemates with their tiny windows like portholes and the thick pillars supporting the low ceiling reminded one of the between-decks in a boat full of immigrants.[4]

In all the Underground Citadel provided accommodation for 6,000 men among its 4,000 metres of passageways, and its bakery and kitchens produced rations for 28,000 men per day.[5] After the war one of the chambers hosted the ceremony to select one of eight Unknown Warriors for ceremonial entombment at the Arc de Triomphe in Paris. The remaining seven are interred with a further 5,000 French soldiers in the *Faubourg Pavé* National Cemetery on the eastern outskirts of the town. The ceremony is recreated in the Underground Citadel, which is open to the public and features a mini-railway tour through other chambers with life-size dioramas of life in the citadel and trenches during the battle.

The Battlefield

The scenes of the fighting immediately prior to and during the Battle of Verdun lie relatively short distances to the west, north-east and south-east of the town. The following sections will each deal with the fighting on the flanks of the Verdun salient in 1915, the struggle for the heights west of the River Meuse and finally the scene of the longest and most intense period of fighting on the east bank of the river. The main sites are fairly well signposted and easily accessible by road. The Mort Homme, for example, now boasts a proper tarmac access road and car and coach park within a short walk of the memorials and monuments on the summit. When the author first visited the site in 1989, this involved negotiating an unmade, hardcore-reinforced track that posed a severe threat to the suspension of his Vespa motor scooter.

With regard to maps, the Michelin 1:200,000 series (1 centimetre = 2 kilometres) is highly recommended and provides detailed coverage of all the major and minor sites. The basic format for this series is the yellow-covered concertina-style *Carte Routière et Touristique*, which is widely available in bookshops and similar outlets in France and the UK. Full coverage of the whole area covered by this guide requires sheets 56, 57 and 62. The mapping is also available in a handier, book form as the *Atlas Routière et Touristique*, which is available in at least two sizes and in bound and ringbound formats. More detailed coverage is available from the IGN (*Institut Géographique National*) 1:25,000 (1 centimetre = 250 metres) Cartes de Randonnée, which are widely available in France. Designed for walkers, these are recommended for visitors intending to take advantage of the network of trails and footpaths that criss-cross the battlefields. Sheet no.3112 ET, *Forêts de Verdun et du Mort-Homme: Champ de Bataille de Verdun* provides coverage of the town of Verdun itself, the main battlefield north-east of the town, and Côte 304 and the Mort Homme. Sheet no. 3012E covers the Butte de Vauquois on the western side of the

16　The 1,100m approach road to the summit of Côte 304.

17　The Memorial at the summit of Côte 304. The inscription reads *Aux dix mille morts héroïques dont sang impregna cette terre* (To the ten thousand heroic dead whose blood impregnated this earth). Note the unexploded ordnance at the base of the monument.

18 Colonel Driant's *poste de commandement* (command post) in the Bois de Caures. The bollards along the front of the bunker bear decorative coats of arms and the names of Driant's officers from the 56th and 59th *Battalions Chasseurs à Pied.*

19 The remains of trenches running to outlying positions in the *Bois des Caures* from Colonel Driant's command post.

20 A German bunker constructed after the battle alongside the D125, a few metres from Colonel Driant's command post.

21 The monument to the 56th and 59th *Battalions Chasseurs à Pied* on the west side of the D905, 100 metres or so from Colonel Driant's command post.

22 Colonel Driant's original grave, where he was interred by a German officer who found his body; the same officer passed the colonel's personal effects to Driant's wife via neutral Switzerland with a letter of condolence.

23a and b Colonel Driant's grave and monument on the spot where he was killed. The inscriptions read *Ici est tombé le Lt. Colonel Driant* (here fell Lieutenant-Colonel Driant) and *Ils sont tombés silencieux sous le choc comme une muraille* (they fell uncomplaining under the shock like a defensive wall).

24 The German cemetery at Ville-devant-Chaumont, a kilometre or so north east of the Bois des Caures. Many of the graves therein date from the initial fighting in February 1916.

25 The *Monument du Soldat du Droit* on the junction of the D913 and D913d leading to Fort Douaumont.

Verdun salient, while Sheet no.3213O does the same for the Les Éparges ridge on the eastern side.

The East Flank

The eastern shoulder of the Verdun salient was formed when the Germans seized the Les Éparges ridge, fifteen miles south-east of Verdun, on 21 September 1914. The ridge, which was 1,500 yards in length and 1,000 feet high, provided a commanding view north-west toward Verdun and the Germans rapidly turned it into a fortress with five distinct defensive lines. The French established a presence on the western slopes of the ridge in October 1914, and in January 1915 GQG decided it would provide a good base from which to eliminate a German foothold across the River Meuse to the south. French engineers thus began to drive mine tunnels under the German lines to support an attack by the 13th and 106th Régiments d'Infanterie.

The attack began with the detonation of four mines under the German positions at 14.00 on 17 February 1915, and by the late evening the 106th *Régiment d'Infanterie* had secured the resultant 100-foot-deep craters despite fierce German counter-attacks. The regiment lost 300 dead, 1,000 wounded and a further 300 missing in three days of fighting. French attacks on 18, 19 and 27 March were less successful and the Germans blew a series of counter-mines, some containing twenty to thirty tonnes of explosive. The French finally captured an intermediate peak midway up the ridge after three full-scale attacks beginning on 4 April 1915, again at heavy cost. The 25th Battaillon de Chasseurs à Pied lost 474 men, and the 67th *Régiment d'Infanterie* 1,029 killed, wounded and missing.[6] In the event, the summit at the eastern tip of the ridge, dubbed Point X, remained in German hands until September 1918. The mine warfare of 1915 drastically and permanently altered the topography of the Les Éparges Ridge by tearing almost a score of huge craters out of the crest and slopes.

Leave Verdun on the D903 toward Metz, and follow it for 14km (9 miles) to Haudiomont. Farther east the road runs through Mars-la-Tour, Rezonville and Gravelotte, which were the scene of fierce fighting during the Franco-Prussian War of 1870–71. Numerous memorials to the fighting are signposted off the main route. In Haudiomont turn right onto the D54 and follow it under the A4-E50 Autoroute to a T junction. Turn right onto the D21 and follow it for 500 metres or so into Muravaux Mont-Villers, then bear left onto the D154. Follow that road through Mesnil-sous-Les Côtes and on into Les Éparges. From there the road to the Éparges ridge and associated monuments is signposted. The road runs east for a few hundred metres toward a large French military cemetery, then hairpins sharply and climbs up the spine of the ridge. Part way up the road doglegs slightly to the left, away from a small car park at the base of a steep log stairway leading up to the 'Ghosts' monument dedicated to the dead and missing of the 106th *Régiment d'Infanterie* on 17–19 February 1915. It consists of a forbidding head rising from a mound of stylised earth studded with skulls, fronted by a relief metal casting of a poilu assisting a wounded comrade. It was inspired by *Académie Française* novelist Maurice Genevoix's work entitled Ceux de '14 (Those of 1914), which was based on his service as a second lieutenant with the 106th *Régiment d'Infanterie*.

The road climbs on past the intermediate peak and along the lip of several huge mine craters, the scale of which has to be seen to be fully appreciated. It terminates at a small car park at the summit, and passes two additional monuments, the *Mémorial du Coq* dedicated to the 12th *Division d'Infanterie* and one to the *Anciens du Génie* (sapper or engineer veterans). A path runs east for a hundred yards or so from the car park to Point X, through a grove of trees planted amid grassed-over craters and trenches that snake away into the woods on either side. The trees obscure the view toward Verdun, but the panoramic vista over the Woëvre Plain graphically illustrates why the Éparges ridge was considered so vital by both sides. Point X also houses a memorial dedicated to the 10,000 men still interred in the clay of the hill, with plaques dedicated to specific French units that fought on the Ridge. A steep, railed footpath runs down from just behind the memorial to the base of the ridge, where it intersects with other footpaths running through the woods that now cloak the Ridge. These are clearly signposted with distances to the various points, and an overall map and details of the battle are posted on a large information board located in the car park. German trenches and the remains of concrete shelters are still clearly visible cut into the steep slope, and a there also a number of concrete shelters. The most impressive is the intact *Abri du Kronprinz* (Crown Prince's Shelter), a long structure boasting several doors set into the hill.

26 The rear aspect of Fort Douaumont. Note the firing slits and openings into the casemates, and the large plaque dedicated to the French troops who retook the fort in October 1916. The fort superstructure is accessible via a footpath just off the right side of the picture.

27 Fort Douaumont's retractable 155mm gun turret, jammed just above ground level.

28 Fort Douaumont's retractable twin 75mm gun turret (right) and the armoured observation dome used to control the fort's guns.

29 Close-up of Fort Douaumont's twin 75mm gun turret. Note the muzzles of the 75mm guns and the rectangular sighting slit between them.

The West Flank

The western shoulder of the Verdun salient lies fifteen miles west and slightly north of the town. Leave Verdun on the N3 toward Reims. Follow it through Regret and Maison Rouge and look out for a turning on the left onto the N35 toward Bar-le-Duc. This road, which was an unmetalled single-track route in 1916, is the famous *Voie Sacrée* (Sacred Way). Along with the Meusien narrow-gauge railway that ran parallel to it, the *Voie Sacrée* was the main supply artery for transporting troops and supplies into Verdun after the Germans severed the main rail lines running south and west from the town. One of General Philippe Pétain's first acts on taking command at Verdun on 25 February 1916 was to check the condition of the route and ensure that the necessary resources were provided to keep the flow of men and supplies running. At this time 3,500 motor trucks were employed on the route between Verdun and Bar-le-Duc, as described by an American war correspondent:

> The one sight of the battle at Verdun that will always live in my memory is that of the snow-covered and ice-coated road north of Bar-le-Duc constantly filled with two columns of trucks. Some were moving north, the others south, and their swaying and lurching progression was comparable to that of young elephants… For long hours at night, I have watched the dim lights of all these trucks, winding their way from north to south like the coils of some gigantic and luminous snake which had no end to it.[7]

As this description makes clear, the *Voie Sacrée* was a continuous twenty-four hour, seven days a week operation, a system named noria after the French word for an industrial bucket water-wheel. An anonymous French driver graphically described the strain this involved:

> On arriving… we did the journey [from Bar-le-Duc to Verdun] twice almost without stopping: that is to say, 48 hours without sleep and almost without eating. I do not know if you can imagine what it means to drive one of these lorries weighing five tons and carrying an equal weight in shells, either during a descent of 12 or 14 per cent and with a lorry just in front and one just behind, or driving during a frosty night, or without lights for short intervals when nearing the front. Can you see a driver alone in his lorry, whose eyes are shutting when a shock wakes him suddenly, who is obliged to sing, to sit very upright, to swear at himself, so as not to sleep, not to throw his lorry into a ravine, not to get it stuck in

the mud, not to knock to pieces the one in front? And then the hundreds and hundreds of cars coming in the contrary direction whose lights blind him! If you can imagine all this, be happy that you can spend your nights comfortably in bed.[8]

It is worth noting that the trucks involved lacked even basic amenities taken for granted today, such as pneumatic tyres, windscreens, heaters and power steering, leaving the drivers exposed to the elements and reliant on brute strength to control their unruly charges. Primitive as they were by modern standards, such vehicles were far from commonplace at the time; there were only 170 motor trucks in the whole French Army in 1914. By the time Pétain took command in February 1916 the officers in charge of the route, Major Richard and Captain Doumenc, had, by commandeering vehicles across the length and breadth of France, increased the fleet to 3,500. A mint condition Berliet truck of the type employed on the *Voie Sacrée* can be seen on display on the lower level of the memorial museum at Fleury.

The road was divided into six sections, each of which had its own dedicated mechanics, repair workshops, engineers and repair gangs. At 10,000 strong, the latter were equivalent in strength to an infantry division, and many of them were drawn from the French colonies in Indo-China and Senegal. These men used a quarter of a million tons of stone in maintaining the carriageway, working the same round-the-clock system as the truck drivers, often by shovelling gravel directly under the wheels of the moving trucks which then acted as road rollers. At its peak 50,000 tons of materiel and 90,000 men per week were flowing along the *Voie Sacrée* into Verdun on 12,000 trucks, one of which passed any given spot at a rate of one every ten to fourteen seconds.[9] The flow of traffic was ruthlessly maintained. Broken-down trucks were unceremoniously tipped off the road for repair and recovery teams to deal with, and horse and foot traffic was banned altogether. The heavily laden poilus were thus obliged to march through the fields alongside the road, and Second Lieutenant Raymond Jubert of the 151st *Régiment d'Infanterie* described the marked contrast between those going up to the line and those coming out:

The first crowd are young, their uniforms brand new; their faces and hands are clean; they look as though they were decked out for a celebration, but their aspect is sad, their eyes dream, they are silent like men who have been abandoned to their fate. The second lot are dirty, scruffy; they have black hands and faces; compared with the others they look like

30 One of Fort Douaumont's retractable machine gun turrets in the raised position; note the armoured observation cupola for controlling the gun's fire to the right.

31a and b (*above*, and *opposite, top*) A preserved trench, marked with lengths of angle iron, in the area dubbed the 'Deadly Quadrilateral' south and west of Fort Douaumont. The area saw heavy fighting after the fall of the fort to the Germans in February 1916. The trench runs along the south side of the D913d before veering north and continuing on the other side of the road.

32 French bunker in the Deadly Quadrilateral, on the north side of the D913d.

33 The Douaumont Ossuary from the junction of the D913 and D913d by the *Monument du Soldat du Droit*.

34 The eastern end of the Ossuary. Note the shape of the 46m tower, designed as a stylised artillery shell.

35 One of the glass panels located around the base of the Ossuary to permit visitors to view the remains within.

36 The 15,000 grave *Cimetière National* in front of the Ossuary, viewed from the top of the tower. The grey building at the top centre of the picture is the Memorial Museum at Fleury.

37 The rear of the east-facing barrack block at the *Ouvrage de Froideterre*. Note the retractable machine gun turret on the left.

38 The business end of the north-west facing *Casemate de Bourges* at the *Ouvrage de Froideterre*. Each opening housed a 75mm filed gun on a special swivelling mount, examples of which can be seen on display outside the Memorial Museum at Fleury.

39 View of the *Ouvrage de Froideterre* from atop the *Casemate de Bourges*. The barracks and machine-gun turret are on the right of the picture. The original north-east facing work is in the centre and runs off the left side of the picture. The work's retractable twin-75mm gun turret is visible on the skyline, with the entrance lower and to the right. Note the shell craters.

40 The retractable machine gun turret (centre) and armoured observation cupola (lower and to the left) located at the left-hand end of the *Ouvrage de Froideterre's* main work. The work is accessible via the entrance door just visible in the centre right of the picture. Again, note the shell craters.

outcasts. But their faces are cheerful; they sing; they wouldn't change their situation for anything, yet they have a kind of pity for the men in those fine uniforms whose paths they are crossing.[10]

The thirty-mile length of the *Voie Sacrée* is currently maintained as a national memorial by the French government. It was inaugurated as such on 21st August 1922 by President Raymond Poincaré and what had been an unmetalled track was reclassified as Route National 35 on 30 December 1923. Its special status is marked by special kilometre stones topped with cast metal replicas of the *Casque Adrian* (Adrian helmet) worn by French troops during the First World War. The helmet was named after the Supply Department official who ordered its adoption and production. The replicas on the kilometre markers are surmounted with laurel leaves, and the markers proclaim the *Voie Sacrée* above another laurel leaf on two of their four faces; the remaining two note the distance to Verdun and Bar-le-Duc. An impressive Memorial sits on a rise just off the junction between the N35 and N3. Constructed from light sand-coloured stone, it consists of a tall central column bearing a stylised image of a winged truck, flanked by two wing walls bearing relief panels depicting trucks, horse-drawn transport and marching infantry moving to and from Verdun.

To reach the western shoulder of the Verdun salient, continue on the N3 from the junction with the N35 *Voie Sacrée* through the villages of Blercourt, Dombasle-en-Argonne and Récicourt. Three kilometres beyond Récicourt look for a right turn onto the D946, and follow that road for 6km (3½ miles) through Aubréville, Neuvilly-en-Argonne and on to Boureuilles. Carrying straight on will take you to the picturesque town of Varennes-en-Argonne, where Louis XVI was recaptured after fleeing the revolutionary regime in Paris in 1791; the Musée d'Argonne in the town also houses a section on mine warfare. The town is overlooked by the massive Pennsylvania State Memorial, erected to honour the US soldiers who liberated the town in September 1918. There are two more US memorials in the area. Montfaucon-en-Argonne, 10km (7 miles) east of Varennes along the D19, houses the American Memorial, a 58-metre-tall tower overlooking the ruins of Montfaucon village topped with a Statue of Liberty. A viewing platform at the feet of the statue can be accessed via 234 steps in the column, and offers a superb view over the battlefield. The Meuse Argonne American Cemetery is located at Romagne-sous-Montfaucon, 10km north of Montfaucon. Extending across 52 hectares, the cemetery is the largest American graveyard in Europe, and contains 14,246 graves including

486 unidentified soldiers. The names of a further 954 missing are recorded on stone panels in the cemetery's Memorial Chapel.

In Boureuilles look for a right turn onto the D212, which runs for a kilometre and a half into the village of Vauquois, located at the base of a steep wooded hill called the Butte de Vauquois. The village was built after 1918; the original village of 168 inhabitants which stood atop the 295-metre-high Butte was totally eradicated by the most intensive mine warfare in history. Vauquois was evacuated on 3 September 1914, and the 82nd *Régiment d'Infanterie* from the 9th *Division d'Infanterie* occupied the hilltop on 15 September. They were driven off by troops from Infanterie Division 33 nine days later at a cost of 200 casualties. The Germans swiftly realised that their new possession offered a matchless observation post over the French lines, including the mainline railway linking Verdun to Reims. Thus German artillery fire controlled from atop the Butte de Vauquois was instrumental in severing this important supply line. They consequently set about fortifying it with their customary speed and efficiency. French attempts to regain the hill began in October 1914 and a series of attacks by the 10th *Division d'Infanterie* between 17 February and 4 March 1915 at a cost of 3,000 French dead and missing. The attacks left the French holding the southern half of the village, with the front line running between the ruined buildings lining its main street. Holding the exposed line was a dangerous business in itself, as this French officer's account of a German artillery barrage on the Butte de Vauquois on 20 February 1916 shows:

> My poor 11th Company falls from the stalk, it falls from the stalk! Eleven more wounded, three of them already dying… My most experienced gunners, the good comrades who survived last winter, the best Boche-killers, are getting wiped out along with the rookies.[11]

However, the bulk of the fighting at the Butte de Vauquois either took place or was initiated from underground. Pionier Bataillon 30 had begun excavating tunnels into the Butte on 7 January 1915, and the first French mine was detonated on 3 February 1915. The depth and scale of the mines then escalated rapidly. At the beginning charges averaged between five and 1,500 kilograms, and were buried from five to fifteen metres deep. Within twelve months they had expanded to an average of fifteen tonnes, placed up to forty metres deep. The Germans detonated a 4.7-tonne mine on 3 March 1916, and a twelve-tonne French response later that month totally destroyed the village church. The largest mine was a German sixty-tonne charge detonated on 14 May 1916 that blew out the whole

41 Close-up of the twin-75mm gun turret at the *Ouvrage de Froideterre*. The damage to the armour appears to have been inflicted by a high-velocity armour-piercing weapon, and may therefore have been inflicted after the 1916 fighting.

42 The Memorial Museum at Fleury, constructed on the site of the village railway station.

43 French Model 1877 155mm gun of the type massed on the west bank of the River Meuse by Pétain, on display outside the Memorial Museum at Fleury. They wrought great carnage by firing into the flank of the German advance on the opposite bank, and were a prime factor in the German decision to expand the battle frontage to include the Mort Homme and Côte 304.

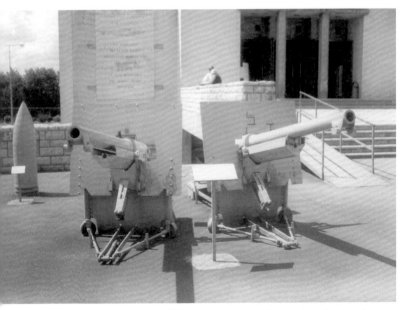

44 French Model 1897 75mm field guns on the special mountings developed to allow standard guns to be emplaced with a minimum of modification in the *Casemate de Bourges* added to many of the forts and ouvrages at Verdun. The steel rails for these mountings can be seen concreted into the floor of the *Casemate de Bourges* at the *Ouvrage de Froideterre* and Fort Vaux.

western end of the hill, killing 108 French soldiers from the 46th *Régiment d'Infanterie* and digging a crater 250 feet wide and sixty feet deep. Another German mine on 24 February 1917 erased the last signs of human habitation on the hilltop by destroying the village well and the sole surviving chestnut tree.

By this point the hilltop had been reduced to a string of huge, interlinked craters up to eighty metres wide and ten to twenty metres deep, with the front-line trenches running along the rims of the craters, in places incorporating the foundations of vanished buildings. The two final charges were a French mine detonated in March 1918 and a German camouflet blown on 9 April. In all, over 500 separate charges were detonated in the Butte, either mines intended to destroy positions on the surface or smaller charges called camouflets, which were designed to collapse enemy tunnels and workings. Seventeen kilometres of tunnels were burrowed out of the hill, with chambers to house barracks, stores, infirmaries, electrical generators and compressors to channel air to the deepest tunnels; the French took to naming their galleries after Paris Metro stations. The Germans withdrew from the Butte de Vauquois on 14 April 1918, and the hilltop was liberated without a fight by troops from the US 35th Infantry Division on 26 September 1918, almost exactly four years after it was occupied by the Germans.

Today the top of the Butte de Vauquois can be accessed in two ways. Pedestrians can use a steep staircase, flanked by two small-calibre French trench mortars, that rises from the village main street. Vehicular access is via a road that joins the main street to the left, and leads to a small car park at the western end of the Butte. The car park has an information board with details of the site, and a truck and a small section of the narrow-gauge railway used to move spoil and materiel underground is on display nearby. The car park is also the meeting point for the guided tours of the hilltop and some of the underground workings run by volunteers from the *Association des Amis de Vauquois et de sa Région*. These are run on the first Sunday of every month, and on specific days in May and September. Special tours can also be arranged for parties of ten or more. Precise details are posted on the information board or can be obtained from the organisation's website, which also has a useful photo gallery.

A wide, curving walkway leads up from the car park through the trees to the hilltop. A wide trench leading to some of the mine workings runs off on the right about halfway up; the author came face to face with a young deer there on his last visit to the site in 2005. The walkway skirts the south edge of the huge crater created by the German mine of 14 May 1916 before emerging onto the hilltop. The crater is eighty metres across and twenty metres deep, and large chunks of masonry from destroyed buildings project from the sides and bottom. A memorial in the shape of a light tower has been erected from pale grey stone on the site of the old village hall, dedicated to the men killed in the fighting there; an estimated 8,000 missing are believed to be entombed in the hill. A larger than life-size French infantryman, swathed in a greatcoat and holding a hand grenade, is carved into the rear side of the tower. The outlook to the south is obscured by trees, but crossing the crater line via a handrailed path to the German held side offers a panoramic view over the lower ground to the north, and shows why both sides considered the Butte a prize worth fighting for.

A German concrete bunker is half hidden by the trees at the eastern end of the hilltop, and it is interesting to speculate exactly how it was constructed. The fact that the French front line lies within grenade range, mere metres away across a mine crater, suggests that the concrete was mixed elsewhere and bucketed up to the site. This can have been no mean feat, however, for not only do relatively small bunkers require surprisingly large amounts of concrete, but the hillside falls away not far from the vertical all along the German side of the hill. Moving west, a section of German trench has been preserved, running through the foundations of long destroyed build-ings; the sides of the trenches have been reinforced with bricks in places, along with logs and wickerwork panels. On a sunny summer day, with no sound except the buzz of insects, it is difficult to imag-ine the reality of 1915–18 for the men holding the trenches across the hilltop. The 'normal' hazards of artillery and snipers must have been bad enough, but the fear that an enemy mine might erupt at any moment beneath your feet must have added a whole additional dimension of psychological stress.

The West Bank of the Meuse

The main battle for Verdun was fought on the east bank of the River Meuse from the latter half of February 1916, but by the beginning of March the fighting had spread to the western side of the river. To access the west bank battlefields, leave Verdun on the D38 from the northern edge of the town, through Thierville-sur-Meuse. Now

45 German 250mm *Minenwerfer* (literally 'mine-thrower') trench mortar. Capable of throwing a 94kg projectile for 1,000 metres or more, this was one of three essentially similar weapons that were also produced in 76mm and 170mm calibres. The base plate could be mounted on wheels – note the stub protruding from the side – and a removable trail allowed it to be deployed like a conventional field piece. The sockets visible on the front and rear of the base plate are for poles used when moving or siting the weapon in the confines of the trenches.

46 The Wounded Lion monument dedicated to the 130th *Division d'Infanterie* at the Chapelle Sainte-Fine crossroads. The monument marks the high point of the German advance toward Verdun on 12 July 1916. The glacis of Fort Souville slopes up in the trees behind the monument.

47 The author in 1990 beside a monument to a French light infantry unit at the site of Vaux village, not far ear the Chapelle Sainte-Fine crossroads. The inscription reads *À la mémoire des trois officiers, onze sous-officiers, cent deux caporaux et chasseurs du Premier Bataillon de Chasseurs à Pied tués sur cette position en arretant l'attaque allemande du 31 mars 1916* (To the memory of the three officers, eleven NCOs and 102 corporals and chasseurs from the 1st Battalion Light Infantry killed in this position while halting a German attack on 31 March 1916).

48 The monument to French War Minister and Minister for Veterans' Affairs André Maginot, a kilometre south-west of the Chapelle Sainte-Fine crossroads on the D112. Maginot suffered a disabling knee wound while serving with the 44th *Régiment d'Infanterie* at Bezonvaux, north-east of Fort Douaumont, on 9 November 1914. The figures represent the bonds of front-line comradeship, the shield is symbolic of Maginot's work in defence of France and the stone wall evokes the Maginot Line defence works that bore his name. The glacis of Fort Souville is hidden in the trees behind the monument.

49 The *Faubourg Pavé* National Cemetery on the eastern outskirts of Verdun on the D112 that leads to the Chapelle Sainte-Fine crossroads, with the Meuse Heights in the background. 5,000 men are buried there, including the seven unsuccessful candidates for France's Unknown Soldier, marked by the large cross in the centre of the picture.

50 The German field guns on display at the main entrance to the *Faubourg Pavé* National Cemetery.

51 Memorial to French non-combatants executed by the Germans during the Second World War, located by the entrance to the *Faubourg Pavé* National Cemetery.

52 The main entrance to Fort Souville. The arched entrance on the left is fronted by a concrete moat. The fort can also be accessed via the guard house on the right, and the fort superstructure can be accessed via the path running alongside it.

53 The rear aspect of Fort Vaux. The dark patch to the right of the small tree in the foreground is the tunnel entrance to the fort's lower levels. The fort interior can be accessed today via a small shop in the casemate by the sign at the extreme left of the picture.

54 *Above, Left*: A memorial plaque on the rear wall of Fort Vaux dedicated to *Pigeon Voyageur du Commandant Raynal* No.787-15, on behalf of the *Colombophiles Morts pour la France* (the pigeon fanciers who died for France). Carrier Pigeon No.787-15 carried the last request for help from the fort's commander, Major Sylvain-Eugene Raynal, on 4 June 1916, and died after delivering the message to Fort Souville; it was rewarded with a posthumous *Légion d'Honneur*.

55 *Above, right*: Memorial plaque on the rear wall of Fort Vaux dedicated to *Les Defenseurs du Fort du Vaux* (The defenders of Fort Vaux).

56a and b The flanking machine-gun galleries at the north-east and north-west corners of Fort Vaux's moat.

57 The upper portion of Fort Vaux's armoured 75mm turret resting in the moat where it was blown from its housing by the sympathetic detonation of a demolition charge. A piece of the mounting ring can be seen alongside the path in the centre right. The concrete wall on the right is the support column for the fort's observation cupola, which is just out of shot. The height of the exposed concrete gives a good indication of the depth of earth that originally protected the fort's carapace, which was blown away by near-constant shellfire.

58 The view north from atop Fort Vaux. Thiaumont Ridge runs along the skyline, with the tower of the Ossuary projecting in the centre of the picture.

59 Fort Tavannes: the gateway leading to the outer courtyard.

60 Fort Tavannes: tunnel linking the outer and inner courtyards.

61 Fort Tavannes: main entrance in the inner courtyard.

62 Fort Tavannes: inner courtyard.

a suburb of Verdun, Thierville was a separate village in 1916. After 2 kilometres the run bends sharply to the right, whilst a minor road carries straight on past a large industrial plant. The minor road is well surfaced, and after another kilometre forks at a large farm, with the surfaced section angling left and an unmade track angling to the right; both run up to a wooded crest. The unmade track is negotiable by car with care, and leads to a small wood that conceals the remains of a small fortification called the Poste de la Belle Épine. As with many of the military remains, it is marked with danger signs. A fire-break provides an unbroken field of view down to the River Meuse to the east and up the ravines cutting into the Meuse Heights across the river.

This crest is the Bois de Bourrus Ridge, and it was the reason for the Germans spreading their attack to the west bank of the Meuse. To the east of the Poste at the tip of the Ridge lies Fort Vacherauville; to the west, accessible via the surfaced track, lie Fort de Marre and Fort de Bois Bourrus. These fortifications were perfectly placed to pour artillery fire into the flank of the German advance down the opposite side of the River Meuse, and the French reinforced their effectiveness by packing in more guns, especially to the north in the lee of the Mort Homme Ridge. These guns extracted a terrible toll from the German infantry formations across the Meuse. They were instrumental in stopping a major German attack on the Côte de Talou hill in its tracks, and also interfered with German artillery; General Lotterer, the German 3rd Corps's artillery commander, was killed by a shell fired from these guns. The Germans therefore launched a corps-scale attack with fresh troops on 6 March, aimed at securing the Mort Homme ridge and the Côte de l'Oie (Goose Ridge) which ran east from it down to the Meuse.

To reach the Mort Homme return to the D38 and follow it east toward Charny-sur-Meuse. The incline down to the village provides an excellent view of the Heights across the Meuse, before the road bends ninety degrees left toward Marre and then again into Chattancourt. The Côte de l'Oie is directly ahead overlooking the road as you approach the latter bend, although the Forêt Domaniale du Mort Homme which now blankets the whole area make it difficult to differentiate the Mort Homme from the Côte de l'Oie. As contemporary maps show, the Mort Homme was unforested at the time of the battle, apart from a few small woods like the Bois de Corbeaux and Bois de Cumières. In Chattancourt the peak of the Mort Homme, sometimes rendered as Point 295, is clearly signposted, and a minor road runs for a kilometre or so up the ridge to a small coach and car park just below the summit. The car park has a large information board with details of the 1916 fighting, and directions for the *Sentier de Cumières et du Mort Homme*. This woodland footpath loops around the spine of the ridge as far as the preserved ruins of Cumières, which was totally destroyed in the fighting, and thus traverses the scene of the most intense fighting. The ground under the conifer canopy is pitted with craters and the remains of trenches, and strategically placed orientation tables provide additional information.

The primary thrust of the initial German attack on the Mort Homme came from the front line 4 kilometres to the north, roughly where the Forêt Communale de Forges now stands. The French reinforced their own line after detecting German preparations, and despite the German opening barrage being among the heaviest seen in the war to date the French counter-bombardment, thickened by the guns massed around the Bois de Bourrus Ridge, blunted their advance short of the Mort Homme. However, the French were caught unawares by what was originally intended to be a subsidiary attack. The German 7th Corps crossed the River Meuse between Brabant and Champneuville on the east bank, assisted by an armoured train sneaked almost up to the front line; this provided close-range fire support until French counter-fire forced it to withdraw. The Germans rapidly cleared and occupied the villages of Forges and Regneville on the west bank. They also pushed up and along the Côte de l'Oie to Point 265, the eastern peak of the Mort Homme ridge, and penetrated into the Bois de Corbeaux that linked the two ridges. By nightfall on 7 March they had occupied the whole wood, inflicted over 3,000 casualties on the 67th *Division d'Infanterie*, and were in a prime position for a further push to seize the remainder of the Mort Homme ridge.

They were prevented from doing so by the arrival and prompt action of Lieutenant-Colonel Macker and his 92nd *Régiment d'Infanterie*. The 92nd had been in reserve, camped under near constant snow in a wood near Dombasle-en-Argonne, 14 kilometres west of Verdun and roughly the same distance south of the Mort Homme. On 6 March the regiment marched in sub-zero temperatures to a wood near Esnes-en-Argonne in the lee of the Mort Homme, spent a night with no shelter and then moved to a stand-by position near Chattancourt, again with no shelter or field kitchen. From there it was ordered to retake the Bois de Corbeaux at 07.00 on 8 March. This entailed another sleepless night, for the regiment began its move up to the start line at 03.00. The line was literally that, for the speed of the German advance had left no time for digging trenches, and it was 900 metres from the German line in the edge of the Bois de Corbeaux according to the Regimental history.

The Regiment advanced with all three battalions in line, led by Lieutenant-Colonel Macker in person, unarmed except for a cane and smoking a cigar, under German fire the while time. When intense German machine gun fire began to tear serious gaps in the French line at 200 metres from the wood, the pace was increased to double time, which unnerved some of the German defenders who began to withdraw. At 100 metres Macker ordered a charge which overran the Bois de Corbeaux and penetrated into the adjacent Bois de Cumières. The 92nd reported its objective secured at 07.20, and Macker issued the following congratulatory Order of the Day:

> Officers, NCOs, Corporals and Soldiers of the 92nd and of the 1st Company of Brigade machine gunners: Today you have, with magnificent élan, executed a superb counterattack, on a flat ground of more than 800 metres and under a terrible hurricane of fire. The enemy has not been able to hold in the face of your valiant effort. I can only find one thing to say to thank you, and that is that I have lived, thanks to you, the most wonderful hour of my life as a soldier. France has the right to be proud of the 92nd.

This, the near suicidal courage of Colonel Macker and his men's determination to close with the bayonet, provides a textbook example of the doctrine of offensive *à l'outrance* (roughly 'attack to the extremes') that permeated the French Army before 1914. However, élan and courage were simply not enough to ward off the power of the German artillery and superior numbers, and the 92nd was slowly but surely forced to give ground. Colonel Macker led his by then depleted regiment in another counter-attack at dawn on 10 March that regained the Bois de Corbeaux and temporarily stabilised the situation, but then his luck ran out. He was killed by a German machine gun after going forward to congratulate one of his battalion commanders. A rapid German riposte then recaptured the entire Bois de Corbeaux after intense fighting which reduced one German battalion to 300 men. The Bois de Corbeaux and Bois de Cumières have been subsumed into the larger forest that now covers the ridge, but the place where Lieutenant-Colonel Macker and the 92nd *Régiment d'Infanterie* performed their gallant deeds is near the picnic area at the north-eastern tip of the Sentier de Cumières et du Mort Homme.

This pattern of attack and counter-attack set the tone for the subsequent fighting on the Mort Homme, which became a murderous game of king of the hill with neither side able to gain a decisive advantage despite the loss of tens of thousands of lives. The Germans launched a renewed assault in the middle of March 1916 and again at the beginning of April. German artillery fired off seventeen trainloads of ammunition in preparation for the latter attack, which finally succeeded in reaching what the Germans thought was the summit of the Mort Homme, albeit at horrendous cost: one German division alone lost 2,200 men in the process.[12] It must have been heartbreaking for the lead German troops to discover that their cartographers were in error, and that the real crest lay another 30 metres up the slope. The following account of a French counter-attack by Lieutenant Raymond Jubert of the 151st *Régiment d'Infanterie* provides a graphic illustration of what the fighting on the Mort Homme involved:

> We assembled without a word. Having put down our knapsacks, we took an ample supply of cartridges, as well as rations for one day. To gain time, my company, disregarding the communication trench moved ahead over the open terrain in single line. Passing the first crest, we descended toward the ravine where, as in a crucible, the deadly explosions and fumes were concentrating in a hellish racket. Another hundred feet and we were in the danger zone. The German shells were raining around us, and the men were silent. They kept marching on, grim faced and in good order, toward the barrier of fire and steel that rose before us.
>
> As I glanced back to make sure my men were following me, the explosion of a shell threw a soldier high up in the air. He fell on the edge of a fresh crater, dead. Half a section had been thrown to the ground, but the men soon got up; after a brief moment of anxiety and fear they quickly and instinctively formed line again... 'We'll give them hell!' a man shouted at me, smiling. 'Darn bastards, they won't be spared.' More voices rang out, a sign of growing confidence. Smiling at my men I calmed them with a gesture. We'll sing, up there. Keep going, my boys! It was deeply gratifying to lead such an assault, and to defy death in such perfect order.
>
> Beyond the crest, however, there was another crest, and we could still see no enemy trenches... When, about five yards to our left, a machine gun suddenly opened fire against us, one of my men began singing, a café-concert hit. He was soon joined by the whole company... other machine guns entered the fray... I heard cries, but began charging ahead and shouted 'Keep in line!'... Our line rushed onward, reached the crest and jumped into a trench which, to our great surprise, was empty – but full of corpses.
>
> At nightfall, and for the next thirty hours, we sustained a violent bombardment. By regaining the lost crest, we had restored the momentarily broken

continuity of our front line. When, after a period of rest, we returned to the Mort-Homme on May 20th, the lines were still unchanged.[13]

The trenches captured by Lieutenant Jubert and his men were soon full of water too, for the German attack of 9 April was followed by a period of heavy rain that forced a two week pause as the terrain turned into glutinous mud under their feet. The Germans took the opportunity offered by the bad weather to prepare a further effort to take the Mort Homme. This included excavating two mile-long tunnels, dubbed 'Gallwitz' and 'Kronprinz', to protect German troops moving up to the line in safety. This was doubtless welcome, but did little to alleviate what faced the troops once they left their front-line trenches and shell holes when the attack was resumed in May. The following French eyewitness account of a German attack illustrates the horrendous price paid by the German troops as they pressed forward up the denuded slopes of the ridge:

At this moment the German curtain fire lengthened... The Germans attacked in massed formation, by big columns of five or six hundred men, preceded by two waves of sharpshooters. We had only our rifles and our machine guns, because the 75's could not get to work. Fortunately the flank batteries succeeded in catching the Boches on the right.

It is absolutely impossible to convey what losses the Germans must suffer in these attacks. Nothing can give an idea of it. Whole ranks are mowed down, and those that follow them suffer the same fate. Under the storm of machine gun, rifle and 75 fire, the German columns were ploughed into furrows of death. Imagine if you can what it would be like to rake water. Those gaps filled up again at once. That is enough to show with what disdain of human life the German attacks are planned and carried out.[14]

Another member of the 151st *Régiment d'Infanterie*, Private Pierre Rouquet, described the ferocity of the German shellfire during the German May attacks:

You couldn't describe the deluge of fire that swept down on us. I was conscious of being in danger of death every second... I ended up stupe-fied. I got the impression that my brain was jumping about in my skull because of the guns. I was completely KOd by the severity of the noise. At the end of fifteen days we came back down, seven to eight kilometres from the front... We had one quiet night's sleep; just one, that's all, then the next day the battalion that had relieved us was wiped out... There were five or six left out of a whole battalion, no more.

We were sent up again with all speed to face another bombardment, one worse than ever. The shells of the 210s were coming over four at a time and we were being buried with every volley. Men were being completely entombed. The others dug them out... My moment came on the stroke of seven o'clock. It was my turn to be buried and you must understand I suffered greatly because being unable to move I could do absolutely nothing. I remember saying 'Well, that's it at last!' and I lost consciousness. I was dead. And then I was being disinterred with picks and shovels and they pulled me out, totally exhausted. My captain... sent me to a first-aid post two kilometres back... I was evacuated. I gathered I stayed four days in a corner, exhausted, in total shock.[15]

The Germans finally secured Point 295 on the crest of the Mort Homme on 29 May 1916, after eighty-four days of near continuous fighting. Today a monument dedicated *Aux Morts de la 40e DI* (To the Dead of the 40th *Division d'Infanterie*) stands just off the slip road into the car park. The summit is a few yards further uphill, and is now a peaceful if slightly brooding place, with trimmed grass verges and wooden benches for the visitor. The brooding quality was highlighted and reinforced by an incident on the author's first visit to the hilltop in 1989, on a clear and very hot July day. First was the slightly unsettling matter of an elderly gentleman who passed one of our party at the bottom of the road where the car park is now located, but did not pass anyone at the top. Even worse was the seeming result of a friend ducking into the trees for a much-needed toilet break after several hours on the road. In less time than it takes to tell, the clear azure blue sky turned dark pewter grey complete with forked lightning worthy of a horror film. This was more than sufficient to prompt a rapid withdrawal down the ridge, during which the heavens opened in yet another flash storm like several others experienced during our journey from Calais. The arrival of this storm was doubtless a matter of pure coincidence, but still a bit too coincidental given the isolated and brooding air of the hilltop.

This atmosphere is heightened by what stands at the centre of the clearing that marks the summit of the Mort Homme. This is, in the author's opinion, one of the most disturbing but appropriate monuments anywhere on the entire Verdun battlefield; du Squelette (Skeleton), dedicated to the dead of the 69th *Division d'Infanterie*, which suffered heavy casualties in the 1916 fighting. The monument consists of a larger-than-life skeleton, presumably representing Death himself, rising erect from the earth cradling a furled standard in his left arm, and with the right arm raised menacingly to the sky. It is mounted on a double plinth inscribed with the words *Ils n'ont pas passé* (They did not pass). This is a play on the slogan 'Ils ne passeront pas!' (They shall not pass!), widely used at Verdun and immortalised by General Robert Nivelle in a famous Order of the Day in June 1916. It is sometimes erroneously attributed to Pétain, who two months earlier had coined his own rallying cry by paraphrasing Joan of Arc: *Courage! On les aura!* (Courage! We will beat them!). All these slogans have become an intrinsic part of the Verdun story.

The fighting on the Mort Homme prompted a further westward extension of the fighting front, once again by the Germans in an attempt to block French flanking fire. This time the French guns were emplaced on a small hill three kilometres west of the Mort Homme called Côte 304, after the height of the summit above sea level. Aimed at the Bois d'Avocourt to the north-west of Côte 304, the attack began on 20 March 1916 and secured the wood in four hours flat taking almost 3,000 of the demoralised French defenders from the 29th *Division d'Infanterie* prisoner in the process. Further progress was then delayed for two days by torrential rain, which gave the French time to recover and reinforce. A renewed German attack on 22 March was rebuffed with over 2,000 casualties, and a French counter-attack six days later only managed to regain a small corner of the Bois d'Avocourt at similar cost.

To reach Côte 304 return to Chattancourt and follow the D38 east toward Esnes-en-Argonne, where Lieutenant-Colonel Macker and the 92nd *Régiment d'Infanterie* spent their freezing, hungry and sleepless night before moving up to meet the German advance along the Côte de l'Oie. The road approaches the village up a steep incline and doglegs through it via a series of sharp hairpin bends. Although partly concealed by the forest, this is roughly level with the saddle that links the Mort Homme and Côte 304. This was a particularly unhealthy spot in 1916, as recorded by a German officer on serving a ten-day stint in the front line there:

The stench of unburied corpses rises from the ravaged former French trenches. Valuable equipment has been discarded everywhere along the road, weapons, munitions, food supplies, gas masks, barbed wire, grenades and other instruments of war. The last patches of grass are already well behind us and all we can see is a wilderness totally and violently created by explosives. The shell holes merging one into the other testify to the horror of the German artillery fire that preceded our advance and the answering fire of the French guns... News arrives through relays of runners for no telephone line stays intact for more than an hour, the cables are destroyed as soon as they are laid... Chancing their arm, some of our pioneers have crept out and dug trenches and set up barbed wire entanglements… The hill itself was originally partly wooded but by now no more than a few blackened trunks are left visible, and there isn't a green leaf or blade of grass.[16]

A kilometre or so beyond Esnes look out for a right turn onto the minor D18; a memorial to the 173rd *Régiment d'Infanterie* under a tree on the corner of the junction makes a useful marker, as does the large French military cemetery 500 metres further on. Follow the D18 for just over a kilometre into the forest that stretches away left and right, and look for another right turn for the summit of Côte 304.

This road runs arrow straight for 1,100 metres up to the summit, and a pine needle-shrouded moonscape of craters and trenches is clearly visible under the conifer trees on either side of the road. The first time the author drove up it in 1989, the sinister opening to 'Mars, the Bringer of War' from Holst's Planets Suite popped unbidden to mind. The road ends in a circular drive around the base of a tall pillar constructed from large grey stone blocks. The front of the pillar, which faces the approach road, bears the chilling inscription *Aux dix mille morts heroïques dont sang impregna cette terre* (To the ten thousand heroic dead whose blood impregnated this earth) in large block lettering. The rear lists all the French units that fought on the hill. It is not unusual to see rusty unexploded ordnance stacked alongside the monument, awaiting the attention of French military disposal teams. The only official burial on the summit of Côte 304 stands to one side of the monument, a civilian grave bordered with ornate cast-iron posts and chains. It belongs to the forty-year-old Second Lieutenant Georges Fabre, holder of the Legion d'Honneur and Croix de Guerre, who served with the 3rd Mixte Régiment de Zouaves et Tirailleurs and was killed nearby on 18 May 1916. The grave was dedicated to his memory by his wife and daughter.

Despite their rebuff on 22 March the Germans maintained the pressure, and by 8 April their troops had secured the village of Malancourt and were pressing against the foot of Côte 304. A new German offensive on both sides of the River Meuse began on 9 April and the slopes of Côte 304 then played host to the same murderous see-saw as the Mort Homme just to the east. The result was described by a French stretcher-bearer stationed on a rise just west of the hill:

From up there, there was a magnificent and entrancing view stretching from the Argonne to Vaux, but inexpressibly mournful. The ridges that are fought over are completely torn up and as though pock-marked by some disease; between the green and richly wooded banks of the winding Meuse you'd think the hillsides had been ravaged by fire.[17]

In a sense this was true, for the hillsides had been ravaged by remorseless shellfire from both sides. The constant explosions blasted away most of the topsoil and the chemicals and gas poisoned what was left beyond repair. The damage defied post-war attempts to return the land to agricultural use, and the decision was taken to seed the whole area with conifer trees, resulting in the Forêt Domaniale du Mort Homme that blankets the area today. Not all of the damage was wrought by artillery emplaced behind the front lines and the following account by the commander of a German trench mortar unit shows that the shelling cut both ways:

…we took two light Minenwerfers [mine throwers] up to Côte 304. We fired and did a good deal of damage. Grenade after grenade – a great many killed – many terribly injured – blown all over the place. The firing sounds like drums – it goes on and on. There is wonderful visibility from Côte 304 and we can see across No Man's Land to Malancourt and Béthincourt… Our trenches were absolutely smashed. 15,000 shells exploded and 4,000 of them were 21cm grenades. Everything in the munition depot, the station line and road was blown to bits… We had some men wounded – one next to me. They tried to get under cover. Lieutenant Spesshenz had an attack of shell shock. I was just pulling myself together when another shell came over and burst about a yard behind me – a splinter got me in the face. Spesshenz was badly wounded in the right arm. The fighting then finished and we went back to our dugouts and I had to sit down to recover myself. There were 70 men killed in my Company and in the 3rd Company 150, also Lieuts. Jakob and Pezzina. It is remarkable what little damage was done to our trenches. I think it is our good work.[18]

The Germans launched their final effort against Côte 304 on 3 May 1916. The attack was restricted to a frontage of just over a kilometre, preceded by a thirty-six-hour barrage from 500 guns. A French machine-gunner from the 26th *Régiment d'Infanterie* recorded the horrific reality of being beneath such an intense bombardment:

The pounding was continuous and terrifying. We had never experienced its like during the whole campaign. The earth around us quaked, and we were lifted and tossed about. Shells of all calibres kept raining on our sector. The trench no longer existed, it had been filled with earth. We were crouching in shell-holes, where the mud thrown up by each new explosion covered us more and more. The air was unbreathable. Our blinded, wounded, crawling and shouting kept falling on top of us and died while splashing us with their blood. It really was a living hell… We were deafened, dizzy, and sick at heart… our parched throats burned, we were thirsty, and the bombardment seemed endless…[19]

Even then it took the Germans four days of bitter close-quarter fighting to overcome the French defenders, and the summit of Côte 304 was not finally secured until 7 May 1916. In all the battle for Côte 304 is estimated to have cost the lives of 10,000 Frenchmen, as reflected in the grim dedication on the monument that now stands atop the hill.

As at all the key sites at Verdun, Côte 304 has a large information board, erected near Lieutenant Fabre's grave. It provides information on the battle and on another woodland walk, the Sentier de la Côte 304 which runs in a roughly rectangular route for about 6km (c.3 miles) across the western side of the hill. Part of the path runs along the upper contours of the *Ravin de la Gueule à Chevaux* (roughly Horses' Mouth Ravine), the site of particularly heavy fighting. The walk also includes a picnic area at the furthest point from the summit, beside the D18 as it runs north through the forest toward what was once the German lines. Although selective tree harvesting in recent years has permitted more undergrowth, the signs of the fighting are still clearly apparent beneath the conifer canopy. As ever, this is made up of overlapping craters of varying shapes and diameters interspersed with the sinuous remains of trenches, some of which are still well over a metre deep. Alistair Horne noted the paucity of visitors to the battlefields west of the Meuse in the early 1960s, and the situation has not really changed forty-four years on. This is now especially marked in comparison with the situation east of the river, where Fleury, Fort Douaumont and the other sites more immediate to Verdun, the World Capital of Peace, receive a constant stream of visitors from across the world.

Horne also noted the eerie nature of the atmosphere on the west bank heights, and remarked the 'labyrinth of firecuts that crisscross the deserted plantations' were not a suitable place for the nervous to get lost.[20] In the present author's opinion, this has not diminished with time either. In common with the Mort Homme, Côte 304 has a desolate, slightly menacing air which was also reinforced during a visit by the author in 1992 with a small group of friends. Having examined the monument and Lieutenant Fabre's grave, we split up to explore further afield. The author followed the twists and turns of a fairly deep trench for several hundred yards down the slope of the hill, to where the corner of a concrete construction of some kind projected from the side of the trench. As I pondered over what the concrete actually was, I became aware of the prickly back-of-the-neck feeling of being watched. Suspecting one of my companions of playing a practical joke, even though nothing had broken the silence, I turned but there was nobody there. Feeling slightly uneasy, I made my way back up to the summit and emerged into the open at the same time as all my companions, from different directions. A subsequent discussion elicited sheepish admissions that all had experienced the same feeling, and at roughly the same time. Rationally, it is difficult to attribute the incident to anything more than overactive imaginations, but it was a curious and rather unsettling experience nonetheless, particularly given Horne's comment.

The East Bank of the Meuse

The sites on the eastern and western shoulders of the Verdun salient and the heights west of the River Meuse are impressive, and were the scene of appalling bloodletting. The epicentre of the Battle of Verdun lies on the east bank of the Meuse, however, encompassing the area now known as the Coeur du Champ de Bataille (the heart of the battlefield). Codenamed Operation Gericht, which can be translated variously as 'tribunal', 'judgement' or 'execution place', the battle was conceived by Field Marshal Erich von Falkenhayn, Chief of the German General Staff, and was intended to knock France out of the war. This was to be achieved by drawing the French into a battle of attrition that would, in Falkenhayn's words, bleed the French Army to death. Verdun was selected as the target because its symbolic status guaranteed a major French effort in its defence, although the German troops assigned to carry out the attack do not appear to have been appraised of the attritional nature of the operation. Gericht was presented to them as a straightforward attack to seize Verdun.

The German attack was to be launched on a thirteen-kilometre (eight-mile) front stretching east from the Meuse, and preparations for the attack began at the end of December 1915. Around 140,000 troops were earmarked to take part, and special concrete shelters, called Stollen, were constructed to house the assault troops in protected concealment. Ten completely new railways were laid to move the thousands of tons of equipment and stores they required, and the bulk of the French civilian population was forcibly evacuated as a security measure. Much effort was dedicated to the artillery, the primary instrument through which Falkenhayn intended to carry out his bleeding strategy on the French. Over 1,200 guns of various calibres were massed north and east of Verdun for the attack, and 1,300 separate trains brought in 2,750,000 shells, sufficient ammunition for six days of intensive firing. A sophisticated fire plan was drawn up to direct their fire onto the most appropriate French targets. Light and medium pieces were to concentrate on the forward French trenches, while heavier guns were targeted upon French support and artillery positions, lines of communication and fixed fortifications. Positions for the guns were prepared in advance under cover of darkness and left, fully stocked with ammunition, under meticulous camouflage. Some of these positions were sophisticated works of engineering in their own right. This was especially the case with the three highly accurate and long-ranged 380mm naval guns brought in to shell roads, rail links and bridges, some of them miles behind French lines.

One of these impressive installations has been preserved in the Bois de Warphémont, seventeen miles north-east of Verdun beyond the Meuse Heights. To reach it, leave Verdun on the N3 toward Etain. In Etain turn north onto the N18 toward Longuyon, and follow that road through Spincourt and Duzey. This area was the hub of the German logistical and artillery effort mounted to support Operation Gericht, and most of the 1,200 guns massed for the attack were emplaced in the woods visible to the left of the road. After passing through Duzey look out for a brown tourist sign indicating a left turn for the German gun emplacement. A minor road leads to the site in the Bois de Warphémont, which housed one of the 380mm naval guns. The other two were emplaced to the south, in the Bois de Muzeray and Ferme Sorel (Sorel Farm) in the Bois de Spincourt.

Normally mounted on capital ships and with a barrel length of 17.1 metres (56 feet), these guns were nicknamed *Lange Max* (Long Max) or *Brümmer* (Growler). Weighing 750 tonnes, they were capable of throwing a 700-kilogram (1,653lb) shell for 47.5 kilometres (28½ miles). The site has a small car park, and an information board provides details of the guns and the local man responsible for the discovery and renovation of the site. A footpath leads to the gun emplacement. The gun has long since disappeared but the huge circular concrete pit, fifteen metres or so in diameter, in which it was mounted remains. The guns were mounted on a traversable metal platform that also supported the loading mechanism. The same diameter as the pit, this platform sat on a large metal spindle attached to the traversing gear, which was set into the concrete base of the gun pit. The gun's fire control system and electrical systems were set in chambers cast into the concrete walls. A hardened ammunition magazine, basically a concrete-roofed tunnel projecting for a hundred metres or so underground at a shallow angle, is located a few metres to one side of the gun emplacement. A small section of narrow-gauge rail track and a truck used to move shells from the magazine to the gun have also been put on display to one side of the emplacement.[21]

Preparations on this scale were difficult to conceal totally, but they were aided to an extent by the broken and wooded terrain, foggy weather and the actions of the French themselves, who by 1916 considered the Verdun sector to be an irrelevant backwater. Driven more by doctrinal dogma than common sense, 128,000 shells and sufficient guns to equip fifty-four artillery batteries were stripped from the forts and strongpoints that protected Verdun.[22] More serious was the generally complacent attitude of the French troops in the trenches, many of whom had been posted there for a rest after service in more active sectors and were thus disinclined to engage in the hard physical labour required to strengthen their positions. Their general attitude was one of live-and-let-live, as illustrated by a French soldier named Anatole Castex:

> We have almost nothing to worry about, we often play cards and sometimes we have to drop them and jump for our rifles. Bang, bang. False alarm. And back we go to our seats and our cards, our minds completely on the game again.[23]

A French infantry sergeant recorded similar sentiments in mid-1915:

> From their trenches, some two hundred metres apart, French and Germans exchange occasional rifle fire to keep themselves occupied. The artillery exchanges shells which swish high above us. The village is in ruins, but a charming stream runs through it and, miraculously, its church tower is standing. Our normal schedule here is four days in the trenches and four days rest, the one amounting to about the same thing as the other.[24]

Complacency was not universal, however. General Herr, commander of the *Région Fortifiée du Verdun*, made constant but unsuccessful requests for reinforcements. Concern over the poor state of the French front-line positions was also apparent nearer the front. Sixty-year-old Lieutenant-Colonel Émile Driant commanded a composite brigade made up of around 1,200 men from two depleted light infantry units, the 56th and 59th Bataillons de Chasseurs à Pied. They were holding the line in the Bois de Caures, eight miles north of Verdun at the very tip of the salient. That front line commanders were also concerned at the lack of preparation and general air of complacency is clear from Driant's comments to a politician friend in August 1915:

> Should our front line be overrun in a massive attack, our second line is inadequate and we're not managing to build it up: not enough men to do the job, and I add: not enough barbed wire. [original emphasis][25]

Despite this, Driant did a creditable job of the defences in his sector. These consisted of a forward zone, comprising a chain of concrete-reinforced platoon positions, backed up by a support line. Behind this lay the last line of resistance made up of more concrete reinforced positions; these included Driant's command bunker.

Colonel Driant's poste de commandement still stands in the Bois de Caures. To reach it, leave Verdun on the D964 running north along the east bank of the River Meuse toward Stenay and Sedan. Follow the road through the village of Charny-sur-Meuse, Bras-sur-Meuse and into Vacherauville, 7km (4 miles) north of the town. Just before leaving Vacherauville, look for a right turn onto the D905, which climbs quite steeply up into the woods that cloak the top of the Meuse Heights. After 6km (3¾ miles) the road forks on a sharp bend to the right. A car and coach park with a picnic area is located on the right just short of the fork. A large covered notice in the car park provides details of the fighting in 1916 complete with maps and photographs, and of a circuitous woodland walk called the Sentier du Bois de Caures. Colonel Driant's poste de commandement or PC is located on the opposite side of the D905 from the car park entrance, a few metres back from the fork with the D125. It consists of a concrete structure ten metres or so in length, set into the ground with observation slots set just above ground level. The bunker is fronted with a curving row of low bollards bearing decorative coats of arms, and each also bears the name of one of Driant's officers.

Operation Gericht was originally scheduled to begin on 12 February 1916. The French front-line troops spent the nights of 11/12 and 12/13 February on full alert after receiving word of the impending assault from German deserters, but the attack was postponed because the bad weather restricted visibility for the

German artillery observers. The weather cleared on 20 February, and the night of 20/21 February was clear, cold and still, so much so that the French could hear their German counterparts singing, and the rumble of trains behind the lines. The German bombardment, the heaviest in history to that date, began at around 07.00 French time on 21 February 1916 and was audible in the Vosges Mountains, 240 kilometres to the south-east.[26] An officer from the 164th *Régiment d'Infanterie* in the Bois de Herebois at the eastern end of the attack frontage noted:

> The trees are cut down like wisps of straw; some shells come crashing out of the smoke; the dust produced by the upheaval of the earth creates a fog which prevents us from seeing very far. All day, we are bent double. We have to abandon our shelter and go to ground in a deep crater; we are surrounded by wounded and dying men whom we are totally unable to help.[27]

One of Driant's men in the Bois des Caures, Corporal Marc Stéphane, gave a graphic description of the psychological burden inflicted by the German *Trommelfeuer* (drum fire):

> Imagine, if you can, a storm, a tempest, growing steadily worse, in which the rain consists entirely of cobblestones, in which the hail is made up entirely of masonry blocks. Remember that a mere 120, at the point of impact has gathered the same energy and releases, just as instantaneously, the same destructive force as an express train hitting the buffers at 90 kilometres an hour… And we're underneath it, you follow? UNDERNEATH IT, as quiet as Baptists, smoking our pipes, waiting from moment to moment for the inevitable, fatal moment when our wretched carcasses are going to be squashed, flattened, ground instantly to dust.[28]

The physical reality of what happened when these metaphorical cobblestones and masonry blocks struck a human target was horrific:

> A great pile of earth, round, shaped like a pyramid, with a hole gouged out all round. Sticking out of it, symmetrically, to a distance of about 40 centimetres, were legs, arms, hands, and heads like the bloody cogs of some monstrous capstan.[29]

With a short pause at around midday intended to draw the French defenders out of their shelter, the bombardment went on for nine hours. Over that period the shells fell at a rate of up to forty per minute, and in the final hour this increased in places to around 80,000 shells per 5,000 square metres. When it lifted from the French front-line positions at around 16.00, Corporal Maurice Brassard of the 56th Bataillon de Chasseurs à Pied reported that 'out of five poilus, two have been buried alive in their shelter, two are more or less wounded, and the fifth is waiting his turn.'[30] It was then that German fighting patrols began to filter forward on the eight-mile attack frontage to assess the damage to the French defences. Wearing white armbands for quick recognition, some carried oxyacetylene cutters to deal with the tangles of French barbed wire. They were surprised to meet resistance, and confused fighting went on through the night.

The traces of this horrendous bombardment are clearly evident in this section of what in 1916 was a patchwork of smaller woods like the Bois des Caures, Bois de Herebois and Bois d'Haumont. Today, partly as a result of the damage inflicted during the fighting, the whole area is covered by the Forêt Domaniale de Verdun, which extends seventeen kilometres (eleven miles) north of Verdun with an average width of eight kilometres (five miles), an area of approximately 136 square kilometres (85 square miles). The Sentier du Bois de Caures traces a circuitous route from Driant's poste de commandement for roughly five kilometres through the woods. It traces the French front line and takes in the site of Beaumont, one of nine villages totally destroyed in the fighting that were never rebuilt after the war and are now commemorated with monuments. The area north of the command post also contains a number of large German concrete bunkers built in 1917 and 1918. These are generally identifiable by small shield-shaped plaques cast into the concrete over the entrances bearing names like *Büffel* (buffalo), *Nashorn* (rhinoceros) and *Walfisch* (whale).

The main German advance began at midday on 22 February 1916, after another five hours of mind-numbing shellfire. By this time Driant's force had been reduced to an estimated 300–400 effectives. Driant rallied his stunned and deafened men, rifle in hand, shouting 'We're here, it's our position, and we're not moving from it.' Later, standing in full view of the advancing Germans, he scornfully dismissed calls from his men to take cover with the response 'You know very well they've never hit me yet!' Thus inspired, the survivors of the 56th and 59th Bataillons de Chasseurs à Pied put up a stubborn resistance, fighting hand-to-hand with rifle butts and even stones when their ammunition ran out. Despite such desperate courage, the weight of numbers began to tell and by the mid-afternoon of

22 February Driant was besieged in his command post, under direct fire from two field guns the Germans had manhandled through the shattered woods. After a conference with his surviving officers, Driant decided to withdraw in order to preserve the lives of his surviving men, who by this time numbered somewhere between eighty and 118. Driant divided his band into three, and led one group through the gathering gloom himself. Sergeant Jules Hacquin was an eyewitness to what happened next:

I had just fallen into a shellhole when a sergeant who was accompanying Colonel Driant and was walking a pace or two in front of him fell in the same hole. This sergeant, he told me afterwards, was called Coisnes and he belonged to the 56th Chasseurs. After having seen the sergeant jump in the hole, I distinctly saw Colonel Driant on the edge of the same hole throw out his arms exclaiming 'Oh! My God!', then he made a half turn and collapsed behind the hole, facing the wood... we could see the colonel. He gave no sign of life, blood was flowing from a wound in his head and also from his mouth. He had the colour of a dead man and his eyes were half closed. The time must have been about 16:30 hrs.[31]

A memorial to Lieutenant-Colonel Driant and his light infantrymen from the 56th and 59th Bataillons de Chasseurs à Pied has been erected on the west side of the D905, 100 metres or so south of the poste de commandement. It consists of a tall standing stone with a carved relief cross, mounted on a stepped, rough-hewn plinth backed by a flagpole. The plinth is set in a raised circular space accessible by half a dozen steps, and backed by a low semi-circular wall. A dozen standard French grave markers belonging to Driant's men killed in the fighting on 21–22 February 1916 are spaced evenly along the wall, and two stone benches are set into the ends of it. Driant's grave is located a few hundred yards away in a wide firebreak in the forest. The firebreak can be reached from the car park via a wooden footbridge and a short path through the trees; alternatively it opens onto the D905 almost opposite the memorial to the 56th and 59th Bataillons de Chasseurs à Pied. Originally the colonel was interred by the Germans deeper in the woods and the grave still exists complete with headstone, indicated by markers. In a gesture harking back to a more chivalrous age, the German officer who found Driant's body on the battlefield not only arranged for him to receive a proper interment, but also passed the colonel's personal effects back to his wife via neutral Switzerland, accompanied by a letter of condolence.

Lieutenant-Colonel Émile Driant is buried where he fell under the eyes of Sergeant Hacquin, having been relocated from where his German opponents laid him to rest with some ceremony in 1922. The grave is marked with a large, light grey stone, surmounted with seven dressed stones arranged in a stepped quoin. One side bears the inscription *Ici est tombé le Lt. Colonel Driant* (Here fell Lieutenant-Colonel Driant). The other side bears the legend *Ils sont tombés silencieux sous le choc comme une muraille* (roughly: they fell uncomplaining under the shock like a defensive wall).

Take the D905 back to Vacherauville, and then turn left onto the D964 toward Verdun. In Bras-sur-Meuse look for a left turn onto the D913, and follow this minor road up again onto the Meuse Heights. The D913 runs through the middle of the *Coeur du Champ de Bataille*, the first sign of which comes up on the left where the road curves south after about 4km (2½ miles). The *Tranchée des Baïonnettes* commemorates a group of soldiers from No. 3 Company, the 137th *Régiment d'Infanterie* who, legend has it, were buried alive at their posts by the German bombardment during the fighting near Thiaumont on 12 June 1916. The commander of the 137th discovered their bodies in 1919 while investigating the disappearance of No.3 Company, in a stretch of trench with a rifle and bayonet projecting from the earth next to each.

The legend does seem a little unlikely, as it is difficult to envisage the circumstances capable of burying around fifty men simultaneously, and it more likely that the soldiers were simply buried in the trench post mortem, the rifles being used as improvised markers. Whichever, the discovery caught the public imagination at the time and a wealthy American benefactor donated sufficient funds to preserve the site for posterity, and the result was ceremonially opened by President of the Republic Alexandre Millerand and the US ambassador in December 1920. The memorial is fronted by a concrete gateway leading to a paved walkway, and consists of a thick concrete roof erected over a stretch of the backfilled trench. Gaps between the rectangular support pillars allow visitors to see a row of rifle muzzles projecting from the earth, each backed by a simple white cross marked *Soldat Français inconnu* (unknown French soldier).

The area behind the *Tranchée des Baïonnettes* memorial was the scene of desperate fighting in the opening days of the battle, as the German advance pushed remorselessly south from the Bois des Caures. By midnight on 24 February, after two days of exposure to German artillery and infantry attacks, the 51st *Division d'Infanterie* had suffered 6,396 casualties and the 72nd *Division d'Infanterie* 9,828. The physical and mental toll the fighting exacted from the

poilus is clear from an eyewitness account of survivors from the
51st Division:

> These men were no longer men, and to recognize men in us kindled
> a flickering light in their eyes, ready to die out again. They were more
> desperate than men shipwrecked at sea or lost in the desert, than men
> buried alive in a mine or a submarine, because they knew that we were
> not saving them and that they would return, after we had fallen, to this
> vast burial amid the iron rain. I remember one man above all, a great big
> fellow, thin and bent over. With his goatskin coat, his eight day beard,
> his grey hands, his eyes as vacant as a prisoner's, he made me think of
> Robinson Crusoe. Yes, we were Robinson Crusoes, poor people engulfed
> in the chaos, that we ourselves had unleashed.[32]

The D913 then crests a ridge just south of the *Tranchée des Baïonnettes*
memorial. 300 metres down the slope look for a left turn onto the
D913d, just where the road curves to the right; the junction is marked
by the Monument du Soldat du Droit, a larger-than-life representation of a poilu in full equipment reclining on a plinth. The D913d
terminates at the car park behind Fort Douaumont. Completed in
1913 at a cost of over six million francs, Fort Douaumont was one of
the most sophisticated pieces of military engineering in the world.
Although originally intended to be the keystone of Verdun's defence,
by 1916 the fort had been stripped of most of its weapons and garrison, to the extent that it fell on 25 February 1916 to a single German
NCO named Kunze who found his way inside almost by accident.
The machine gun gallery where he entered can be seen in the fort's
defensive ditch, and the fort's internal courtyard is accessible from
the car park, which boasts the usual information board, via a set of
steps and a long earthen ramp. The badly eroded rear wall of the
fort has been repaired with fresh masonry in places, but the damage
inflicted by a French 400mm railway gun on 23 October 1916 is still
clearly visible. This was noted at the time by a war correspondent
from the UK Daily Telegraph newspaper, Ellis Ashmead-Bartlett,
who visited the fort shortly after it had been recaptured by North
African troops from the *Régiment d'Infanterie Coloniale du Maroc* on
24 October 1916:

> Especially interesting was the spot in the upper galleries where the 400
> mm shells had entered. Dawn was breaking and the pale light was shin-
> ing through this arch cut out of the solid concrete by these heavy shells.
> Sentries stood guarding the aperture which was rapidly being put in a state
> of repair. You look out and beyond on to a sea of huge shell craters. There

are no luxuries or comforts of any sort for the garrison, for it has only been possible to carry up the bare necessities of life and a reserve supply of ammunition. I made my way through all these long galleries, damp, cold and filthy and studied the heroic defenders. They are great fellows, these Chasseurs. They are cold and caked with mud and weary from the incessant labour of carrying up supplies, but ever determined and indomitable. They have got back the fort and will never give it up again.[33]

Douaumont's superstructure can be accessed via paths at either end of the inner courtyard. The right-hand path also leads to the larger of the fort's two retractable gun cupolas, containing a 155mm piece, the armoured dome jammed slightly askew just above ground level. The other, mounting a short 75mm gun, can be reached via the foot-worn paths that criss-cross the glacis of the fort. The 75mm turret is centrally placed, with an armoured observation dome set a few metres to its front. A combination of shelling – the whole of the superstructure is pitted with craters – and almost a century's worth of erosion has exposed the concrete underpinning of the turret, showing the thickness of earth originally piled atop the fort for protection. The view from the superstructure is extensive, and illustrates why it was constructed on that spot. Fort Vaux is clearly visible to the south-east, as is the Bois des Caures to the north, and the immediate front is occupied by a French Army firing range for anti-tank weapons.

The interior of the fort is also accessible for a small fee via the souvenir shop which occupies one of the casemates that line the rear face of the fort. Visitors are provided with an information clipboard and are allowed to follow the marked circuit at leisure. The rear casemates were originally used for accommodation, and some still contain the iron-framed double bunk beds used by the French Army at that time; another is fitted out as a bakery. The atmosphere in the fort is always cold and damp, and the walls and floor in most parts feature the beginnings of stalagmites and stalactites caused by minerals seeping through the masonry and concrete from outside. Conditions were probably little if any better during the battle, but the shelter of 'Uncle Douaumont' was a much sought-after commodity, as related by a German medical officer named Stephen Westman:

...at an observation post on top of Fort Douaumont one of the telegraphists had been taken ill... I took with me two stretcher bearers... We carried him into the fort and down one flight of stairs after another. Deep in the middle of the fort, protected by many feet of reinforced concrete, the French had built in one of the casemates an operating theatre, of which the Germans made good use. There were always two German surgeons on duty... During the operation [the telegraphist had acute appendicitis] I could feel how the whole fort shook when a particularly heavy shell, most probably with a delayed action fuse, landed and exploded. However, we were safe, and only flakes of whitewash fell from the ceiling... Afterwards I strolled through the fort, with its many dugouts and casemates. The entrance to one of them was bricked up and someone had fixed a plaque, with the inscription 'Here rest 1052 German soldiers' – a whole battalion who were sleeping in the casemate. Apparently one of them had smoked, and barrels of fuel for flame-throwers, which were stored there, had exploded, and not a single soul had survived.[34]

The scene of this incident, at the western end of the fort's wide central corridor, is still marked to this day, with a memorial to the 679 German soldiers killed in an accidental explosion on 8 May 1916; the resultant fire was so fierce that the tunnel had to sealed with the dead still inside. The memorial features a commemorative plaque detailing the event, and a single white cross dedicated to *Den Toten Kameraden* (the fallen comrades). The lower level of the fort is also included in the circuit, via a long concrete staircase, and it is sobering to consider the absolute darkness that would result if the electric lighting failed for any reason. The lower level contains a number of armouries and storerooms, and also allows access to the inside of the retractable gun turrets. These utilised an ingenious weighted cantilever system, and the mechanisms, gun breeches and ammunition-lifting tackle remain an impressive sight despite being frozen by almost a century of rust and neglect.

The area south and west of Fort Douaumont was the scene of heavy fighting after the German capture of the fort, so much so that it was dubbed the 'Deadly Quadrilateral'. The D913d bisects a preserved trench line, complete with information post, and a number of woodland walks radiate out across this area from Fort Douaumont, details of which are posted on the covered information board in the fort car park. Douaumont village, which stood 500 metres west of the fort, was the scene of especially fierce fighting immediately after the fall of Fort Douaumont, as the war diary of the 33rd *Régiment d'Infanterie* recorded:

From six-thirty in the morning, terrible shelling by heavy artillery over the whole breadth of the sector and to a depth of three kilometres. The earth trembled without a pause; the noise was unbelievable. No liaison, either forward or to the rear, was possible; all telephone-wires had been cut and any messenger sent out was a dead man... At about one-fifteen in the afternoon, after a bombardment that had cut the lines to pieces, the Germans launched their attack to encircle the 3rd Battalion... It was then that the magnificent feat was performed. The 10th Company was seen to charge straight forward at the massed enemy reaching the village, engaging them in a terrible hand-to-hand struggle in which these brave men received blows from rifle-butts and bayonets from every side until they were overpowered. Seeing itself completely surrounded, the 10th Company launched itself into a furious attack led by its commanding officer, Captain de Gaulle, charging close-packed bodies of men, selling its life dearly and falling gloriously.[35]

The dramatic and jingoistic language of this account accurately reflects the ethos of the French Army of the time, and thus underplays reality and human cost of the events described. The 95th *Régiment d'Infanterie* was virtually destroyed defending Douaumont village on 25 February, and the 33rd *Régiment d'Infanterie* lost a third of its strength within three days of relieving the 95th. The epic fight described above was alleged to have taken place on 1 March 1916, and the Germans finally secured the village on 4 March after it had changed hands several times. Incidentally, the officer mentioned was the same Charles de Gaulle who led the Free French Forces after 1940 and later became President of France. He was actually captured after being badly wounded, possibly by the blast from one of his own grenades, and spent the remainder of the war in a German prisoner-of-war camp. According to his post-war account to his former colonel, he was wounded while attempting to lead his surviving men to safety, rather than in a last-ditch attaque *à l'outrance*.[36]

Be that as it may, today the site of Douaumont village is occupied by the largest and most impressive monument of all those located on the Verdun Champ de Bataille. Located diagonally opposite where the D913d rejoins the D913 proper, the Ossuaire de Douaumont occupies a section of the crest and reverse slope of the Thiaumont–Froideterre Ridge. Originally the site was occupied by a provisional wooden Ossuary established as a collection point for human remains gathered from across the battlefield. Work on a permanent stone replacement began on 22 August 1920, paid for by a nationwide fundraising effort led by Monseigneur Ginisty, the Bishop of Verdun; the coats of arms of the various cities that contributed are reproduced around the outside of the building. The resultant monument was ceremonially opened on 7 April 1932, although the remains had been lodged therein five years previously. Intended to represent a vertical artillery shell flanked by two horizontal examples the Ossuary is 137 metres long, with the central tower rising to 46 metres. The tower houses a rotating light and a 2,300-kilogram bell and can be accessed for a small fee. The intermediate landings feature glass cases containing uniforms and weapons, and the bell chamber affords a panoramic view across the battlefield, with orientation information etched into the stone sills of the window openings.

The main building features a Catholic chapel with three specially commissioned stained glass windows entitled 'The Offering of Wives and Mothers', 'Stretcher Bearers and Medical Orderlies', and 'The Sacrifice'. Two large sculptures, The Poilu of Verdun and the Statue of Silence, dedicated to the sacrifice of the front-line soldiery and their mourning wives and mothers respectively, are located in separate alcoves. The rear entrance to the Ossuary opens into a book and souvenir shop that features a small cinema. The latter has regular audio-visual presentations on the battle, with commentary in a number of languages via individual headsets. The shop area also features a number of coin-operated 3D viewers containing glass-plate images from the Battle of Verdun and elsewhere. Thanks to the rather less restrained attitude of the French censors, many of the images are graphic in the extreme.

The primary feature of the interior of the Ossuary, however, is the eighteen vaulted alcoves which house two or more polished granite tombs, each of which covers an eighteen cubic metre vault. These vaults contain the remains of unknown combatants recovered from specific sectors of the battlefield, the names of which are inscribed in the wall above the tombs. Individual, unit and corporate memorials to the missing are carved into the stone blocks that make up the walls and vaulted roofs of the alcoves. In the event, the capacity of the eighteen vaults proved insufficient to house all the gathered remains, and an additional 150 cubic metre vault was built into one end of the Ossuary cloister. It is covered by a circular polished granite platform incorporating a Flame of Remembrance. In all, the vaults contain the remains of 130,000 men, which are visible from outside the building via glass blocks set into the masonry, a macabre and somewhat startling touch on first view. The sides and rear of the Ossuary comprise a large car and coach park, whilst the slope at the front down to the D913 is taken up by the *Cimetière National* de Douaumont, containing the graves of a further 15,000 French soldiers. Most are marked with the standard French concrete cross and metal information plaque, but the grave markers of Muslim soldiers feature an ornate representation of a mosque dome and are oriented toward Mecca.

The Thiaumont Ridge was the scene of fierce and sustained fighting in June and July 1916, as the Germans built up to their supreme effort to reach Verdun. Much of the fighting was focussed on a concrete fortification called the *Ouvrage de Thiaumont* and two smaller supporting works called PC118 and PC119, which blocked the northern end of a spine of critical high ground. The 347th *Régiment d'Infanterie* successfully repelled the first German attack on the Ouvrage on 8 June 1916, but the unit was reduced to 365 men in the process. In all the fortification changed hands over a dozen times before the Germans finally secured it on 23 June. Today the badly battered remains of the Ouvrage lies a hundred metres or so from the south-west edge of the Ossuary car park, and marked paths run on to the PCs. This is a section of the *Sentier de Froideterre*, which follows a roughly seven-kilometre circuit around the crest of the Thiaumont–Froideterre Ridge from the Ossuary to the point where the ridge falls away into the Meuse Valley. An account by a German soldier named Anton Steiger, who sheltered in what sounds like one of the PCs, clearly illustrates the conditions both sides endured during the fighting in this area, and how little the reality had changed after over four months of fighting:

> The dugout was an old, half blown in, French casemate about 150 yards away from the fort of Thiaumont. From outside it had looked a mere hummock of earth. The entrance was like that of a fox's hole. At the end of a short passage some broken steps led down into the place we had occupied for four days. Dead bodies were lying under the soil, one of its legs protruding up to the knees. There were three separate chambers down there: one was full of rockets and detonators; another – as big as our kitchen at home – in which we were housed, also contained French ammunition; the third was full of French explosive. It was pitch dark the whole time, as we had only a few candlesticks. There was a horrible smell down there too – the reek of decomposing bodies; I could hardly eat anything the whole four days… On the third day the French artillery opened such an intense fire on the dugout with 28cm guns that we thought it would certainly be blown in altogether… On the fourth day, Friday, the heavy artillery fire started again early in the morning and continued until 9.30p.m. Just think what that means! Ten hours in a dugout under shellfire; ten hours in the expectation of being buried alive, or of being blown through the air if a shell should happen to fall where the explosive is stored…[37]

The conditions changed little after the French reoccupied the area, as Captain Paul Tuffrau noted in his diary in September 1916:

> At 10:30p.m. I go to survey position P.C. 119 near Thiaumont. These plateaux are pounded by shells dropped during the day, but at night they are full of stretcher-bearers bringing back the day's casualties. We walk through Battery C. We wade through mud. Craters filled with water reflect the light every time a rocket is fired. The smell of corpses everywhere.[38]

Not all the fortifications on the Thiaumont–Froideterre Ridge are in such bad repair. Follow the D913 past the front of the Ossuary and when it curves sharply left toward Fleury carry straight on onto the D913b, which runs along the reverse slope of the ridge to the D964 alongside the River Meuse. PC 119 is set back from the road on the right about 500 metres on. After a kilometre there is a small car park on the left for the *Quatre Cheminées* (Four Chimneys), complete with the usual covered information board. The *Quatre Cheminées* was an underground French command post cut into the hillside, ten metres underground and around seventy metres in length. It is named after the four ventilation shafts that projected from the hillside uphill from the entrance; these are easily spotted today thanks to the pointed metal rain covers painted in horizon-bleu. The interior of the shelter can be explored from two concrete tunnel entrances; these are accessible via a railed footpath that runs down the steep slope and around the perimeter of the site. The surface of the command post was overrun by German troops on 23 June 1916 who, unable to penetrate the entrances by the French troops within, resorted to dropping grenades down the ventilation shafts. The occupants were saved by a timely counter-attack by light infantrymen from the 114th Battaillon de Chasseurs à Pied, which drove the attackers off.

Two hundred metres or so further down the D913b from the *Quatre Cheminées* there is a slip road on the right which climbs in a steep curve before ending in what was once the courtyard of the *Ouvrage de Froideterre*. It now boasts a rolled stone car park complete with picnic benches and a covered information board, amid a sea of grass-covered craters. Unlike the *Ouvrage de Thiaumont* at the other end of the ridge, Froideterre is intact and consists of three main works arranged around the courtyard. These are all open for visitors to examine internally, and have concrete steps for access to the their roofs. A long bunker with two retractable turrets, one for a machine gun and the other with twin short 75mm guns, faces north-east. This was the original fortification, and a subsequently added Casemate de Bourges to the left faces north-west, although the gun ports in the staggered front face of the work are oriented north. To the right of the original work is a large concrete barrack bunker for the garrison, which is also open to visitors. The German attack of 23 June 1916 failed to penetrate the Ouvrage, and the German troops who attacked the *Quatre Cheminées* had actually bypassed Froideterre. Nonetheless, the German preparatory bombardment for the attack was extremely heavy, and included 116,000 shells containing phosgene gas, a new and deadly chemical nicknamed 'Green Cross gas' due to the markings on the shells. The barrage was described by a French soldier unlucky enough to endure it:

> Masked, blinded, half-suffocated and half-buried in the earth thrown up by the incessant shell-fire, the troops in the line... knew perfectly well that, when the tornado lifted, that moment would be the signal for the attack. They waited (and what a waiting that was!) on ground churned up by fire, listening to the pitiful cries of the wounded, and with the dead to keep them company. They waited, controlling their nerves, all on edge but strung towards one object, one idea, never to give ground but to fight and hold on. The sentries wiped with their benumbed fingers the glasses of their periscopes and peered into the smoking horizon. The barrage lifts, the enemy are leaving their trenches. 'Ah! Here they come!'[39]

Heavy though the fighting around Froideterre was, the main German thrust was aimed along the spine of high ground running south from the *Ouvrage de Thiaumont* toward Fort Souville. To reach it, head back up the D913b past the *Quatre Cheminées* to the junction with the D913 proper, and turn right. After just under a kilometre on the right there is a small car park for the *Village Détruit de Fleury-devant-Douaumont* (the destroyed village of Fleury). French and German artillery totally destroyed nine villages during the Battle of Verdun, to the extent that there was no effort to rebuild them after the war. In some instances, the only trace of habitation was an odd brick, shards of roof tile or simply a differently coloured smear in the earth. Memorial stones erected on the site they once occupied commemorate eight of these disappeared communities. The ninth, Fleury, was selected to serve as a symbolic memorial for them all, in part because of its central location in the so-called 'Red Zone' where the Verdun fighting reached its height. A village of 400 inhabitants in 1914 on the narrow-gauge Meusien railway line running north from Verdun, Fleury was extensively shelled before the German attacks in June and July 1916. The village changed hands no fewer than sixteen times during those attacks before finally being secured by the Germans on 23 June 1916. By the time it was recaptured by the French in the middle of the following month, the village had been virtually erased from the earth.

Today the only building on the site of Fleury is a small chapel built after the end of the war, where former inhabitants used to meet on an annual basis. This tradition is still maintained by their descendants, and the chapel front was adorned with a religious sculpture entitled Our Lady of Europe in 1979. Fleury also exists as a legal entity, complete with a mayor who represents its interests in Paris. More tangibly, the village is marked with a memorial stone that declares *Ici Fleury-devant-Douaumont Détruit en 1916* (This is Fleury, Destroyed in 1916) over a carved street map. The streets have been laid out as a network of gravel paths which run through the craters and trees planted on the site in the 1930s, complete with street name signs; individual buildings are marked with small pillars bearing metal name plates.

A further 500 metres or so down the D913 stands the *Mémorial de Verdun Fleury-devant-Douaumont*, a two-storey museum erected on the site of Fleury railway station. Inaugurated in 1967, the museum was built with funds raised by Verdun veterans through the Comité National du Souvenir de la Bataille de Verdun (National Committee for the Memory of the Battle of Verdun). The committee was headed at that time by the novelist Maurice Genevoix, who served with the 106th *Régiment d'Infanterie* at Les Éparges. A number of items are on display outside the museum, including a French 155mm gun, two French 75mm pieces on the special mountings developed for use in the Casemate de Bourges, and a German Minenwerfer trench mortar. There are also four blue-painted heavy artillery shells for the German 380mm and 420mm and French 400mm and 520mm guns, which inflicted such damage to the French forts at Verdun; they are all five feet or more tall.

The museum entrance leads into the upper level, the outer walls of which are lined with glass cases filled with uniforms, weapons, equipment, contemporary photographs and other artefacts from the battle. Among the most striking is *La Boue* (The Mud), a sculpture by Alphonse Prévost depicting a poilu attempting to pull a comrade mired up to his waist in a shellhole to safety with his rifle. Two fighter aircraft, a German Fokker Eindecker monoplane and French Nieuport biplane, are suspended from the roof, and a huge map of the battlefield flanked by illuminated information boards covers an entire wall. These are used to give regular presentations on the progress of the battle in French, German and English, the various phases being depicted on the map with coloured lights. The centre piece is an opening in the floor that affords an overview of a life-size diorama of the battlefield, complete with shattered tree stumps, barbed wire and other battle debris including a damaged

German 77mm field gun. The lower level allows a closer view of the battlefield diorama and a number of others, and equipment displays line the outer walls. The latter include a French 75mm field gun, limber and horse team, and a pristine Berliet truck of the type used to carry supplies on the *Voie Sacrée*. The former include a life-size reconstruction of the Pouzargue painting *Vers l'Oubli* (Towards Oblivion), depicting a party of stretcher bearers carrying a dead soldier across the cratered battlefield for burial.

The German advance stalled at Fleury on 23 June 1916, largely due to lack of reserves, and the ruins of the village were the scene of savage fighting as the French made repeated counter-attacks. The main German attack was renewed on 10 July 1916 after two days of torrential rain that almost instantly transformed the parched battlefield into a quagmire. Some German units had spent the interim behind the sparse shelter of the railway embankment running south-west from Fleury station, their every move exposed to the remorseless gaze of French artillery observers. Despite fierce French resistance the Germans advanced some 400 metres into the French defences, and the next day a party from Infanterie Regiment 140 briefly reached the glacis of Fort Souville before being driven off by the fort garrison. This, the high point of the German advance in the Battle of Verdun, is close to the Chapelle Sainte-Fine crossroads, 500 metres south of the Fleury museum where the D913 crosses the D112. It is commemorated by the Wounded Lion monument, a larger-than-life depiction of a supine animal roaring defiance, dedicated to the dead of the 130th *Division d'Infanterie*.

Fort Souville lies hidden in the dense wood behind the monument, and the south-west-running stretch of the D112 toward Verdun is parallel with the front of the fort glacis. A number of memorials to units and individuals who fought in the general area have been erected along this stretch of road, including one dedicated to a Lieutenant Dupuy and the small group from the fort garrison who drove the German interlopers from the glacis of the fort on 12 July 1916. The most impressive, dedicated to former French War Minister and Minister for Veterans' Affairs André Maginot, is located just under a kilometre from the Chapelle Sainte-Fine crossroads. A pre-war politician, Maginot volunteered for service on the outbreak of war, and received a disabling knee wound on 9 November 1914 while serving with the 44th *Régiment d'Infanterie* at Bezonvaux, north-east of Fort Douaumont. He returned to politics in 1916 and was largely responsible for the Maginot Line, a chain of sophisticated fortifications erected facing the German frontier in the 1930s which, although much derided, were never actually penetrated frontally.

With wide stone steps leading up from the road and fronted by a paved area, the monument consists of a large circular shield mounted on a stone wall as a backdrop for a cast metal sculpture of a wounded Maginot being assisted from the battlefield by two comrades. The figures represent the bonds of front-line comradeship, the shield is symbolic of his work in defence of France, while the wall evokes the defence works that bore his name.

The D112 enters the eastern outskirts of Verdun by the walled *Faubourg Pavé Cimetière National*. Although only a third the size of that at the Douaumont Ossuary with 5,000 graves, the cemetery is still an impressive sight, the stark, serried rows of white crosses softened with numerous rose bushes planted alongside them. The cemetery is arranged around a raised square containing the graves of the seven unsuccessful candidates for France's Unknown Warrior, surmounted by a large stone cross. The selection was made at a ceremony in Verdun's Underground Citadel in 1920, and the successful candidate is interred under the Arc de Triomphe in Paris. The path in from the main entrance to the cemetery runs through a memorial garden which features a decorative, six-pointed paved area. A captured German field gun, manufactured by Krupp or Skoda, sits in each point, and a memorial erected in 1947 to French non-combatants executed by the Germans during the Second World War is set by the edge of the memorial garden. An adjacent area contains a memorial to French aviation pioneers Nieuport, Thierry de Ville d'Auvray and Bresson, who were all killed in flying accidents before 1914.

The entrance to Fort Souville can be seen via a wide trail running west from the D913 1.2km from the Chapelle Sainte-Fine crossroads, which emerges onto the D112 west of the Maginot memorial. It can also be reached via a footpath from the Casemate Pamard at the side of the D913 500m short of the trail entrance, which has dedicated car park and information board. (The Casemate Pamard was a type of armoured machine gun emplacement introduced in 1917 as a less complex alternative to the retractable turrets used hitherto.) The interior of Fort Souville is unsafe, although the author once had an interesting conversation with a lone English potholer who emerged unexpectedly from the fort interior despite the sign inscribed *Danger du Mort* (Danger of Death). The stone entrance, complete with concrete wing walls, is intact. It is separated from the path by a concrete moat that must have utilised a drawbridge of some kind, and a flanking guard post with firing slits and internal walls to deflect the blast.

Fort Souville was part of the inner ring of forts protecting Verdun to the north-east, with Forts Douaumont and Vaux comprising the outer ring. The road to Fort Vaux, the D913a, branches from the left side of the D913 a kilometre past the trail leading to Fort Souville. Fort Vaux lies at the end of the 2.5-kilometre-long D913a, on a 340m elevation facing east over the Woëvre Plain. About halfway the road dog-legs around a cutting on the right, where a number of members of the French Resistance were executed by the Germans in 1944. They are commemorated on the *Monument des Fusilées de Tavannes* (Monument to the Shot of Tavannes) which stands to one side of the cutting. Fort Vaux was the scene of an epic siege at the beginning of June 1916, as part of the German preparation for their final assault toward Verdun; Vaux enjoyed a perfect field of fire over the approaches to Fort Souville, three kilometres or so to the south-west.

The fort was commanded by Major Sylvain-Eugene Raynal, a long-serving officer relegated to fortress duties after a sustaining a serious leg wound earlier in the war, and was in less than perfect condition. The fort's single 75mm turret had been destroyed when a near miss from a 420mm shell detonated a demolition charge, and another penetration over one of the corridors linking outlying galleries to the fort proper had been plugged with sandbags. The immediate German pre-attack barrage, which rained shells on the fort at a rate of 2,000 per hour, opened up several more such breaches that were blocked in the same way. In addition, the promise of shelter had attracted 600 men into a work intended to house a third of that number and, unbeknown to Raynal, the fort's main water cistern had been damaged.

After dealing with a number of smaller supporting fortifications, the German assault on Fort Vaux began in the early hours of 2 June 1916. By the late afternoon they had gained control of the fort superstructure, and penetrated the fort's interior via the sandbagged breach. Despite this Raynal and his men held out for five days in the face of repeated German attacks with flame-throwers, toxic smoke and mines, fighting hand-to-hand in the cramped, inky black passageways. In the end it was lack of water that defeated the fort garrison rather than the Germans. Raynal was obliged to reduce the daily water ration to a quarter pint per man on 4 June, and recorded his reaction on being informed that the fort's water reserves were almost exhausted:

> It was in the course of that afternoon [4 June 1916] that the sapper sergeant in charge of the stores came and asked to speak to me in private, and said in a hoarse voice: 'Mon commandant, there is practically no water left in the cistern.' I started, I made him repeat what he had said, I shook him.
> 'There has been dirty work here.'

'No, sir, we have only served out the ration you laid down. It is the marks on the register which have been wrong.'

Then our agony began. I gave orders to hold back the little that remained and to make no further allowance today...[40]

Raynal was not exaggerating with his reference to agony. By the end his men were reduced to licking moisture from the walls; some reportedly resorted to drinking their own urine. Communications with the outside world were severely curtailed after shellfire destroyed the fort's signal station and Raynal sent out his final report via his last carrier pigeon the same day. It took several attempts to get a rather stunned Carrier Pigeon No.787-15 away, and the unfortunate bird expired due to gas poisoning shortly after delivering the report; its dedication to duty was rewarded with a posthumous *Légion d'Honneur*. With no relief forthcoming, virtually out of water and with a number of badly burned and wounded men, Raynal finally surrendered on 7 June. His personal account of the decision illustrates the perennial commander's dilemma:

Had I the right to prolong resistance beyond human strength and to compromise uselessly the life of these brave men who had done their duty so heroically? I took a turn in the corridors. What I saw was frightening. Men were overcome with vomiting... Some lost consciousness. In the main gallery, a man was licking a little wet streak on the wall.

7th June! Day broke, and we scarcely noticed it. For us it was still night, a night in which all hope was extinguished. Aid from outside, if it came, would come too late. I sent off my last message, the last salute of the fort and its defenders to their country. Then I turned to my men:

'It is all over my friends. You have done your duty, the whole of your duty. Thank you.'

They understood, and together in one shout we repeated the last message which my instrument had just sent off: Vive la France!

In the minutes which followed a silence as of death fell upon the fort.[41]

In stark contrast to the near primeval struggle that had preceded it, the surrender was carried out amid chivalric scenes reminiscent of an earlier age. The fort's garrison formed a guard of honour for the German officers despatched to meet Raynal, who handed them ornate ceremonial key to the fort. He was then taken to the HQ of the German 5th Army at Stenay for an audience with Crown Prince Wilhelm; the latter presented him with a sword to replace his own which was lost somewhere inside Fort Vaux. In all, the garrison of

Fort Vaux inflicted 2,742 casualties on the German attackers, at a cost of twenty dead and around a hundred wounded. It was reoccupied by the French without a fight in November 1916.

As at Douaumont, Fort Vaux's courtyard has been filled in to provide a car park, although a sunken section containing the original entrance to the fort's lower level has been retained. The moat is accessible at either end of the fort's back wall, and the machine gun galleries that caused the Germans so may casualties can be seen, complete with the damage inflicted by the German sappers attempting to silence them. The badly cratered fort superstructure is criss-crossed with footpaths, and the small armoured observation dome through which Raynal and his men helplessly watched the German attackers atop the fort is still intact. Pieces of the demolished 75mm gun turret lie nearby, and their size gives a graphic indication of how well armoured the turrets were, as well as the size of explosion necessary to inflict such damage. The badly damaged rear wall of the fort has been repaired to an extent, and bears two large marble plaques. One is dedicated to *Les Défenseurs du Fort du Vaux* (The Defenders of Fort Vaux), and bears the following dedication above a list of the units represented in the fort garrison: 'In this ruined fort 250 men resisted for seven days to 7 June 1916 furious German assaults, with attacks from gas, liquid fire and the torture of thirst'.

The other is dedicated to Pigeon Voyageur du Commandant Raynal No. 787-15, on behalf of the *Colombophiles Morts pour la France* (the pigeon fanciers who died for France). The plaque contains the text of Raynal's last report and the citation for the *Légion d'Honneur* awarded to Carrier Pigeon No.787-15, surmounted by a representation of a pigeon atop an Adrian helmet resting on victor's laurels. Thanks to the efforts of a taxidermist, both bird and medal were displayed in the Les Invalides military museum in Paris. Brass replicas of the pigeon can be purchased in a small book and souvenir shop in one of the fort's casemates, and the interior can be accessed for a small fee. Raynal's command post has been preserved, complete with a contemporary photograph, as has the dovecote where the carrier pigeons were housed, adjacent telephone exchange, the fort infirmary and chapel. The damaged water cistern can be seen sunk into the floor in the main corridor, which has been divided with rough stone intended to deflect blast and act as defence points against the German intruders; the originals were built of sandbags. One casemate contains a grave, complete with a wooden cross bedecked with red, white and blue ribbon. The damage inflicted on the flanking Casemate de Bourges by an underground German mine on 5 June has been repaired, and it contains a 75mm gun on its special mounting.

The damage at Forts Douaumont and Vaux has been repaired to some extent to make them attractive and safe for visitors, and their layout has been altered by the provision of car parks, access ramps and so forth. This is not the case with Fort Tavannes, part of Verdun's inner defence ring located two kilometres due south of Fort Vaux. Apart from almost a century's worth of plant growth and natural deterioration, Tavannes remains in the same battered state the German heavy guns left it in 1916. To reach it follow the D913a back to the junction with the D913 proper, and turn left. After 300m look for a trail leading into the woods on the left. This is the *Sentier de Tavannes et de la Batterie de l'Hopital*, a clearly marked path that loops around Fort Tavannes and takes in a number of outlying works; the Batterie l'Hopital is a hardened artillery position in a loop in the D913 west of the fort.

After 100m or so the track takes a 90 degree turn to the right, with a branch carrying straight on with a warning sign that it leads into a military training area. This branch runs for 70m or so straight to the rear entrance of Fort Tavannes. The gateway is intact albeit with some loose masonry, as is the main courtyard which contains a lot of deadfall, rubble and litter indicating use as a French Army exercise feeding or resupply point. The courtyard is much lower than the surrounding woodland, giving a good idea of what Forts Vaux and Douaumont looked liked before their courtyards were filled in. A narrow sally port tunnel into a small outer courtyard and larger example with staggered blast walls leading into the main court-yard are perfectly intact, as is arched entrance into the fort proper, although the interior looks to be badly damaged and dangerous. Despite the damage and neglect, Fort Tavannes provides a useful insight into what the larger defensive works before Verdun looked like when they were operational.

Fort de Tavannes is on the very edge of the Champ de Bataille, and the D913 only runs for another 700 metres or so south from the entrance to the *Sentier de Tavannes et de la Batterie de l'Hopital* before coming to the N3. Turning left on that road leads to Etain, to the north of which lies the German 380mm gun emplacement just off the N18 in the Bois de Warphémont. Turning right leads back into the eastern outskirts of Verdun, just south of the *Faubourg Pavé Cimetière National*.

Maps

1. *Tranché des Baionnettes*
2. *Ossuary*
3. *Ouvrage de Froideterre*
4. *Quatre Cheminées*
5. *Fleury Museum*
6. *Maginot Memorial*

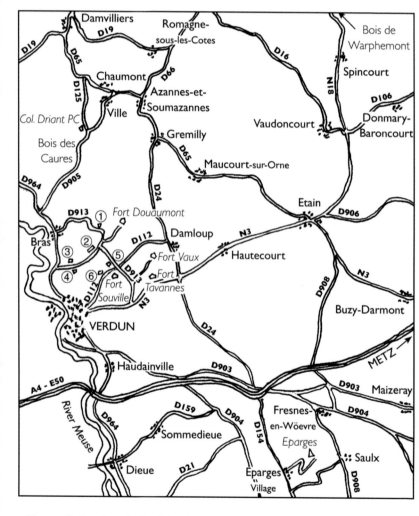

1 The east flank and east bank of the Meuse

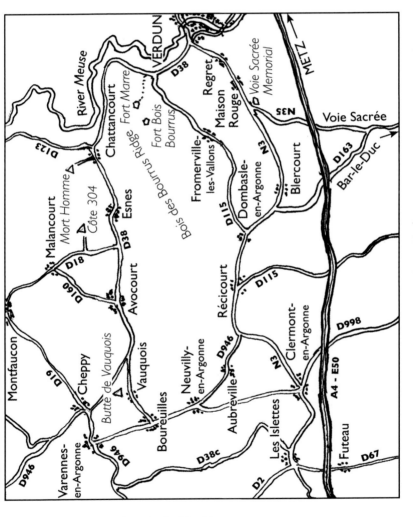

2 The west flank and west bank of the Meuse

List of Illustrations

All photographs are from the author's collection.

Part 1

Part 2

Point X.

12 The steps leading up to the summit of the Butte de Vauquois, flanked by two French trench mortars.

13 The monument *Aux morts de la 40ᵉ DI* (To the dead of the 40th *Division d'Infanterie*) on the peak of the Mort Homme.

14 *Du Squelette* (Skeleton), monument to the dead of the 69th *Division d'Infanterie*.

15 Memorial to the 173rd *Régiment d'Infanterie* at the junction of the D38 and D18 leading to Côte 304.

16 The 1,100 metre approach road to the summit of Côte 304.

17 The Memorial at the summit of Côte 304.

18 Colonel Driant's *poste de commandement* (command post) in the Bois de Caures.

19 The remains of trenches running to outlying positions in the Bois des Caures from Colonel Driant's command post.

20 A German bunker constructed after the battle alongside the D125, a few metres from Colonel Driant's command post.

21 The monument to the 56th and 59th *Battalions Chasseurs à Pied* on the west side of the D905, 100 metres or so from Colonel Driant's command post.

22 Colonel Driant's original grave.

23a, b Colonel Driant's grave and monument on the spot where he was killed.

24 The German cemetery at Ville-devant-Chaumont, a kilometre or so north east of the Bois des Caures.

25 The *Monument du Soldat du Droit* on the junction of the D913 and D913d leading to Fort Douaumont.

26 The rear aspect of Fort Douaumont.

27 Fort Douaumont's retractable 155mm gun turret, jammed just above ground level.

28 Fort Douaumont's retractable twin 75mm gun turret (right) and the armoured observation dome used to control the fort's guns.

29 Close-up of Fort Douaumont's twin 75mm gun turret. Note the muzzles of the 75mm guns and the rectangular sighting slit between them.

30 One of Fort Douaumont's retractable machine gun turrets in the raised position; note the armoured observation cupola for controlling the gun's fire to the right.

31a and b A preserved trench, marked with lengths of angle iron, in the area dubbed the 'Deadly Quadrilateral' south and west of Fort Douaumont.

32 French bunker in the Deadly Quadrilateral, on the north side of the D913d.

33 The Douaumont Ossuary from the junction of the D913 and D913d by the *Monument du Soldat du Droit*.

34 The eastern end of the Ossuary. Note the shape of the 46m tower, designed as a stylised artillery shell.

35 One of the glass panels located around the base of the Ossuary to permit visitors to view the remains within.

36 The 15,000 grave *Cimetière National* in front of the Ossuary, viewed from the top of the tower. The grey building at the top centre of the picture is the Memorial Museum at Fleury.

37 The rear of the east-facing barrack block at the *Ouvrage de Froideterre*. Note the retractable machine gun turret on the left.

38 The business end of the north-west facing Casemate de Bourges at the *Ouvrage de Froideterre*.

39 View of the *Ouvrage de Froideterre* from atop the Casemate de Bourges.

40 The retractable machine gun turret (centre) and armoured observation cupola (lower and to the left) located at the left-hand end of the *Ouvrage*

Endnotes

Part 1

1 See Alistair Horne, *The Price of Glory* (London: Penguin, 1964), p. 56; and *Verdun: Vision and Comprehension*, 6th Edition (Drancy: Editions Mage, 1989), p. 10.

2 Sometimes rendered as Serré de Rivière.

3 See Horne, pp. 17–18; Ian Ousby, *The Road to Verdun* (London: Pimlico, 2003), p. 52; and Anthony Clayton, *Paths of Glory* (London: Cassell, 2003), p. 99.

4 Ousby, p. 53.

5 Figure cited in Malcolm Brown, *Verdun 1916* (Stroud: Tempus, 1999), p. 51.

6 Clayton, p. 99.

7 Horne, p. 119.

8 Troisième Bureau (literally 'third office') was the French Army's operations branch; GQG was the French term for their General Staff Headquarters.

9 Horne, p. 21.

10 Ousby, pp. 28–29.

11 Horne, p. 19.

12 Clayton, p. 38; and Ian Sumner & Gerry Embleton, *The French Army 1914–18*, Osprey Men-At-Arms Series No. 286 (London: Reed International Books, 1995), pp. 13–14.

13 Clayton, p. 38.

14 Horne, p. 20.

15 Clayton, p. 38.

16 Ousby, p. 53.

17 Clayton, pp. 17–19; for a detailed account of the evolution of Plan XVII see Hew Strachan, *The First World War, Volume I: To Arms* (Oxford: Oxford University Press, 2001), pp. 180–195.

18 Strachan, p. 155.

19 Horne refers to 4,278 trains and 1,300,000 men, while Clayton cites 4,300 and 1,500,000; see Horne, p. 24; and Clayton, p. 19.

20 For a detailed account see Clayton, pp. 17–30.

21 Figures cited in Horne, p. 26.

22 James Joll, *The Origins of the First World War*, 2nd Edition. (London: Longman, 1992), p. 98.

23 Figures cited in Horne, p. 27.

24 Clayton, p.58.

25 Ibid, pp.67–73.

26 Richard Holmes, Fatal Avenue: *A Traveller's History of the Battlefields of Northern France and Flanders, 1346 – 1945* (London: Jonathan Cape, 1992) , p.220.

27 Horne, p.56.

28 Holmes, pp.221–222; and *Verdun and the Battles for its Possession: A Panoramic History and Guide* (Clermont-Ferrand: Michelin & Cie, 1920), p.4.

29 Figures cited in *Verdun: Vision and Comprehension*, pp.47–48.

30 Quoted from Holmes, p.222.

31 *Verdun and the Battles for its Possession*, p.5.

32 Horne, p.56.

33 Ibid., p.119.

34 Clayton, p.26.

35 Ousby, p.54.

36 Horne, pp.58–59; and Clayton, pp.99–100.

37 Ibid., p.58.

38 Ousby, pp.55–56.

39 For an account of Falkenhayn's background, prior career and the evolution of Gericht, see Horne, pp.38–47.

40 Quoted from Falkenhayn's December 1915 memorandum to the Kaiser; cited in ibid., p.44.

41 Ibid., p.47.

42 Ousby, pp.40–41.

43 Horne, p.49.

44 Ibid., p.62.

45 Ibid., p.77.

46 Ibid., p.79.

47 Ousby, p.64.

48 Horne, p.85.

49 Ibid., p.87.

50 Ousby, p.69.

51 Horne, pp.95–96.

52 Ibid., p.110.

53 Clayton, pp.85–86.

54 Poilu (hairy): French slang term for the common front-line soldier, due to their unkempt and unshaven appearance; equivalent to the British term 'Tommy'.

55 Quoted in Horne, p.157.

56 Figures cited in ibid., p.166.

57 Clayton, p.106.

58 Figures from Horne, pp.159–161.

59 Figures from ibid., p.178.

60 Ibid., p.180.

61 Entry from the diary of Sergeant Karl Gartner, cited in Brown, p.71.

62 Figures from Horne, p.181.

63 Figures cited in Clayton, p.108.

64 See for example Horne, p.239.

65 Figures cited in Clayton, p.108.

66 Horne, p.237.

67 Figures from Ousby, p.217.

68 Horne, footnote, p.241.

69 Ousby, p.215.

70 Figures from Horne, p.260.

72 Ibid., pp.266–267.

73 For a detailed account see Ousby, pp.229–227.

74 Figure from ibid., p.229.

75 In fact the phrase or something like it was already common currency among the troops at Verdun and probably dated back to the opening stage of the battle in February 1916; see ibid., footnote, p.231.

76 Horne, p.289.

77 Ibid., p.294.

78 Figures cited in ibid., pp.298–299.

79 Ibid., p.300.

80 Ibid., pp.304–306.

81 Ibid., 307–308.

82 Figures cited in *Verdun and the Battles for its Possession*, p.20.

83 Ibid., p.24.

84 Figures cited in Clayton, p.110. These are cited as the most up to date, although Horne refers to French losses totalling between 377,231 and 469,000, and German losses between 337,000 and 373,000; see Horne, p.327.

85 Figures cited in Horne, pp.298–299, 303.

86 Quoted in ibid., pp.302–303.

87 Ibid., p.335.

88 Ibid., p.318.

89 Figures cited in ibid., p.322.

90 Figures cited in Clayton, p.134.

91 Ibid., p.135.

92 Quoted from Horne, p.351.

Part 2

1 Henry Bordeaux, *Douleur et gloire de Verdun, 21 février 1916–2 janvier 1917* (Paris: Librairie Plon, 1957–1959); cited in Ousby, p.62.

2 H. Warner Allen, Special Correspondent of the British Press with the French Armies, The Times, 8 March 1916; cited in Brown, p.120.

3 Diary of Lieutenant Henri Desagneaux, 106th Regiment d'Infanterie, entry for Thursday 15 June 1916; cited in Brown, p.125.

4 René Arnaud, *Tragédie Bouffe, A Frenchman in the First World War*, translated by J.B. Donne (London, Sidgwick and Jackson, 1966); cited in Brown, p.126.

5 Figures cited in *Verdun: Vision and Comprehension*, p.32.

6 Figures cited in *Verdun: Vision and Comprehension*, pp.47–48.

7 Cited in Brown, p.85.

8 Cited in Brown, p.84.

9 Figures from Horne, pp.159–161.

10 Quoted from Raymond Jubert, *Verdun (mars–avril–mai 1916)*, (Paris: Payot, 1918); cited in Brown, p.87.

11 Account by André Pézard, cited in Ousby, p.63.

12 Figures from Horne, p.181.

13 Quoted from Raymond Jubert, Verdun (mars–avril–mai 1916) (Paris: Payot, 1918); cited in Brown, pp.77–78.

14 Quoted from Charles F. Horne (Ed.), *Records of the Great War* (National Alumni, 1923); cited at http://www.firstworldwar.com/diaries/verdun_lemorthomme.htm.

15 Quoted from interview with Private Pierre Rouquet; cited in Brown, p.106.

16 Quoted from a letter by Second Lieutenant Christian Bordeching; cited in Brown, p.107.

17 Extract from Pierre Teilhard de Chardin, *The Making of a Mind* (London: Collins, 1965); cited in Brown, p.75.

18 Extract from the diary of Second Lieutenant W. Weingartner, Minenwerfer Kompanie 38, Jäger Division 38, XI Corps; cited in Brown, pp.107–108.

19 Extract from Richard Thoumin (Ed), *The First World War* (London: Secker & Warburg, 1963); cited in Brown, p.76.

20 Quoted from Horne, p.351.

21 For contemporary photographs, technical details and a table of locations for these guns see M. Luzent's les Canons de l'Apocalypse at http://html2. free.fr/canons/canmax.htm (French language site).

22 Horne, pp.58–59; and Clayton, pp.99–100.

23 Henri Castex (ed.), *Verdun, années infernales: La vie du soldat au front d'août 1914 à septembre 1916* (Paris: Albatros, 1980); cited in Ousby, p.55.

24 Account by Sergeant Étienne Gilson, quoted in Lawrence K. Shook, Étienne Gilson, *The Étienne Gilson Series*, No.6 (Toronto: Pontifical Institute of Mediaeval Studies, 1984); cited in Ousby, p.55.

25 Letter from Driant to Paul Deschanel, President of the Chamber of Deputies; cited in Ousby, p.59.

26 Ousby, p.64.

27 Account by G Champneaux, quoted from Jacques Péricard, *Verdun: Histoire des combats qui se sont livrés en 1916*; cited in Brown, p.46.

28 Marc Stéphane, *Verdun: Ma dernière relève au Bois des Caures* (18–22 février 1916) (Paris, Librairie René Liot, 1929); cited in Ousby, p.66.

29 Quoted from Raymond Jubert, *Verdun (mars–avril–mai 1916)* (Paris: Payot, 1918); cited in Ousby, p.66.

30 Cited in Brown, p.47.

31 Quoted from Jacques-Henri Lefebvre, *Verdun: La plus grande bataille de l'histoire racontée par les survivants* (Verdun: Éditions du Mémorial, 1996); cited in Brown, p.48.

32 Quoted from Jean Bastier, *Pierre Drieu La Rochelle: Soldat de la Grande Guerre, 1914–1918* (Paris: Éditions Albatros, 1989); cited in Ousby, pp.82–83.

33 E. Ashmead-Bartlett, *Some of My Experiences in the Great War* (London, George Newnes, 1918); cited in Brown, pp.151–152.

34 Quoted from Stephen Westman, Surgeon with the Kaiser's Army; cited in Brown, pp.113–114.

35 Quoted from Jean Lacouture, *De Gaulle, The Rebel*; cited in Brown, p.72.

36 See Ousby, pp.104–105.

37 Quoted from Dr Philipp Witkop (Ed), *German Student's War Letters* (Munich, 1928); cited in Brown, pp.134–135.

38 Quoted from Paul Tuffrau, *1914–1918 Quatre années sur le front: Carnets d'un combattant* (Imago, Paris 1998); cited in Svetlana Palmer and Sarah Wallis, *A War in Words: The First World War in Diaries and Letters* (London: Pocket Books, 2003), p.203.

39 Quoted from *Verdun: An Illustrated Historical Guide* (Verdun: Éditions Lorraine, Frémont, n.d.); cited in Brown, pp.128–129.

40 Quoted from Guy Chapman, *Vain Glory* (London: Cassell, 1937); cited in Brown, pp.115–116.

41 Ibid., p.118.

Further Reading

As the endnotes show, the battle history section is largely based on three English-language works. Of these, Horne's *The Price of Glory* remains the best overall account despite being forty-four years old at the time of writing, and is highly recommended to the reader seeking a more detailed but highly readable account. Malcolm Brown's *Verdun 1916* is also a useful work, shorter and easier to digest than Horne, and containing a large number of contemporary photographs and other illustrations. Ousby's *The Road to Verdun*, whilst a mine of information, is perhaps a little oblique for readers looking for a straightforward account of the battle, dealing as it does with the wider cultural background and impact in a thematic rather than chronological manner. Finally, readers looking for a concise yet highly detailed and readable work on the French Army during the First World War could do much worse than Clayton's *Paths of Glory*. The full publisher's details of these works are included in the endnotes. Details of maps are included in the Battlefield Guide section, and the details of other works cited in that section appear in the relevant endnotes.

The following web links are also recommended for readers looking to visit Verdun, or merely looking for additional information. Many sites also feature excellent contemporary and current photographs and other illustrations:

http://www.verdun-tourisme.com/en/index.htm – Verdun's official tourist site, containing everything from a potted history of the town and the 1916 battle to addresses, links and prices for accommodation.

http://www.xs4all.nl/~verdun/ – Dutch-English-language site with numerous pages dedicated to different areas of the Verdun battlefield.

http://www.worldwar1.com/france/vacquois.htm – English-language page with details and photographs of the Butte de Vauquois.

http://www.westernfront.co.uk/thegreatwar/articles/americanperspective/longdistanceguns.htm – English-language article concerning the German 380mm naval guns used at Verdun, with maps, diagrams and photographs. Note: the water-filled emplacement in the Bois de Warphémont pictured has since been restored.

http://www.voie-sacree.com/eng/index.htm – French site with English translation. Details of the *Voie Sacrée* then and now with maps and photographs.

http://www.webmatters.net/index.shtml – English-language site dedicated to he First World War, containing excellent pages on all the key locations of the Verdun battlefield with current colour pictures.

Index

TEMPUS – REVEALING HISTORY

Private 12768 Memoir of a Tommy
JOHN JACKSON

'Unique... a beautifully written, strikingly honest account of a young man's experience of combat' *Saul David*

'At last we have John Jackson's intensely personal and heartfelt little book to remind us there was a view of the Great War other than Wilfred Owen's' *The Daily Mail*

£9.99   0 7524 3531 0

The German Offensives of 1918
MARTIN KITCHEN

'A lucid, powerfully driven narrative' *Malcolm Brown*

'Comprehensive and authoritative... first class' *Holger H. Herwig*

£13.99   0 7524 3527 2

Verdun 1916
MALCOLM BROWN

'A haunting book which gets closer than any other to that wasteland marked by death' *Richard Holmes*

£9.99   0 7524 2599 4

The Forgotten Front
The East African Campaign 1914–1918
ROSS ANDERSON

'Excellent... fills a yawning gap in the historical record' *The Times Literary Supplement*

'Compelling and authoritative' *Hew Strachan*

£12.99   978 07524 4126 9

Agincourt
A New History
ANNE CURRY

'A highly distinguished and convincing account' *Christopher Hibbert*

'A *tour de force*' *Alison Weir*

'*The* book on the battle' *Richard Holmes*

A *BBC History Magazine* Book of the Year 2005

£12.99   0 7524 3813 1

The Welsh Wars of Independence
DAVID MOORE

'Beautifully written, subtle and remarkably perceptive' *John Davies*

£12.99   978 07524 4128 3

Bosworth 1485 Psychology of a Battle
MICHAEL K. JONES

'Most exciting... a remarkable tale' *The Guardian*

'Insightful and rich study of the Battle of Bosworth... no longer need Richard play the villain' *The Times Literary Supplement*

£12.99   0 7524 2594 3

The Battle of Hastings 1066
M.K. LAWSON

'Blows away many fundamental assumptions about the battle of Hastings... an exciting and indispensable read' *David Bates*

A *BBC History Magazine* Book of the Year 2003

£12.99   978 07524 4177 1

If you are interested in purchasing other books published by Tempus, or in case you have difficulty finding any Tempus books in your local bookshop, you can also place orders directly through our website

www.tempus-publishing.com